C000132152

This book belongs to...

Name: James

Age: 10

Favourite player: Jkohnson

Written by Rob and Barbara Mason

A TWOCAN PUBLICATION

ISBN 978-1-909872-25-7

£8

2014-2015 Predictions...

Sunderland's final position: 14th

Sunderland's top scorer: Johnson

Barclays Premier League Champions: Chealse

Barclays Premier League top scorer: costa

FA Cup Winners: Arsenal

Capital One Cup Winners: Sunderland

Teams to be relegated: 18th

19th Leicster

20th qpr

CONTENTS

One of the highlights of the year is the Junior Black Cats' fun day. It's held every year just outside of the Stadium of Light. As you can see from the photographs a great time was had by all, with plenty for everyone to enjoy.

FAMILY FUN

Young Sunderland fans can join the Junior Black Cats free of charge.

Junior Black Cats, Sunderland AFC's official supporters' club for fans aged under 16, is free to join. As a member you will automatically be entered into a competition to win the chance to lead out the team as a matchday mascot*.

Not only that, you will also receive:

- Your own membership card
- A colouring book (ages 0-3)**
- The Junior Black Cats Magazine (ages 4-11)**
- Legion of Light (ages 12-16)**
- The opportunity to attend a Christmas party
- A Christmas card from the players
- The opportunity to attend other SAFC events
- Emails from Samson
- A section on safc.com with competitions, puzzles and downloads

Sign up for FREE at safc.com/juniorblackcats
Call 0191 551 5157 or email juniorblackcats@safc.com

*Mascots are chosen at random from the Junior Black Cats database - age restrictions apply. **UK and Ireland only.

DAY

junior blackcats

THE OFFICIAL SAFC JUNIOR SUPPORTERS' CLUB

Members had a great time with dodgems and a waltzer amongst the fairground rides. There was also a fantastic zip-wire to try if you were brave enough as well as a climbing wall and demolition zone!

For the younger fans there were bouncy castles while the Snow Queen and Mermaid Princess helped with princess lessons and just to keep the party bouncing Heart radio were there with their road-show. As well as all this Foundation of Light coaches put on skills and drills sessions, small sided games and seeing as it was summer, 'football tennis'.

If you were at this year's Family Fun Day see if you can spot yourself on any of these photographs. If you weren't there make sure you don't miss out when 2015's Junior Black Cats' Fun Day comes around.

Costel **PANTILIMON**

BORN: February 1st 1987 **POSITION:** Goalkeeper

INTERNATIONAL: Romania **SIGNED FROM:** Manchester City

PREVIOUS CLUBS: Aerostar Bacau, (Romania), Timosara (Romania), Manchester City.

DID YOU KNOW: Costel is six feet eight inches tall which makes him the tallest player in the Barclays Premier League and the tallest to ever play for Sunderland?

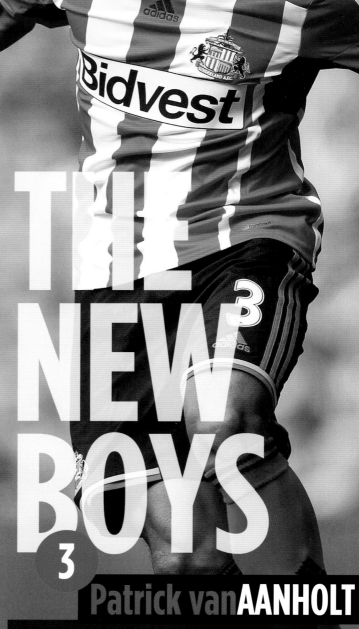

THE NEW BOYS

Patrick van **AANHOLT**

BORN: August 29th 1990 **POSITION:** Left back

INTERNATIONAL: Netherlands **SIGNED FROM:** Chelsea

PREVIOUS CLUBS: Chelsea plus loans to: Coventry, Leicester, Newcastle, Wigan and Vitesse Arnhem (Netherlands).

DID YOU KNOW: Chelsea scored 12 goals in the two Barclays Premier League games that Patrick played for them?

Will **BUCKLEY**

BORN: November 21st 1989 **POSITION:** Winger

SIGNED FROM: Brighton & Hove Albion

PREVIOUS CLUBS: Rochdale and Watford

DID YOU KNOW: When Will signed for Sunderland the only Barclays Premier League side he'd scored against was newly promoted Leicester. He'd scored against the Foxes for Brighton and Watford?

28

Sebastian COATES

BORN: October 7th 1990   **POSITION:** Centre back

SIGNED FROM: Brighton & Hove Albion

INTERNATIONAL: Uruguay   **PREVIOUS CLUBS:** Nacional

SIGNED FROM: Liverpool on a season long loan

DID YOU KNOW: Coates played for Uruguay against England in the World Cup finals in 2014?

27

Santiago VERGINI

BORN: August 3rd 1988   **POSITION:** Centre back or right back

INTERNATIONAL: Argentina

SIGNED FROM: On loan from C.S. Uruguay of Costa Rica

PREVIOUS CLUBS: Velez Sarsfield, A. Paz, Olimpia, Verona, Newell's Old Boys, Atletico Fenix and Estudiantes (loan)

DID YOU KNOW: Santiago played in the same youth team as Ricky Alvarez at Velez Sarsfield?

20

Ricardo ALVAREZ

BORN: April 12th 1988   **POSITION:** Midfielder / winger

INTERNATIONAL: Argentina

SIGNED FROM: Internazionale on a season long loan

PREVIOUS CLUBS: Velez Sarsfield

DID YOU KNOW: Two days after signing for Sunderland Ricky played for Argentina as they won 4-2 in Germany?

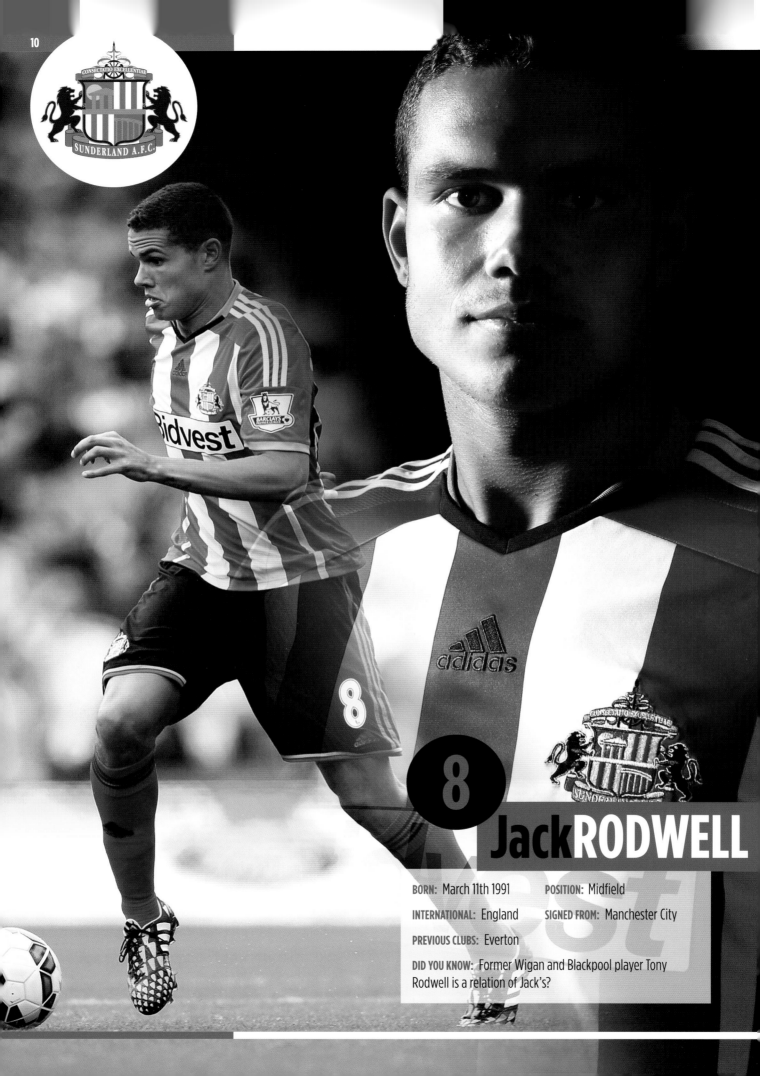

Jack RODWELL

8

BORN: March 11th 1991 **POSITION:** Midfield

INTERNATIONAL: England **SIGNED FROM:** Manchester City

PREVIOUS CLUBS: Everton

DID YOU KNOW: Former Wigan and Blackpool player Tony Rodwell is a relation of Jack's?

Billy JONES

2

BORN: March 24th 1987

POSITION: Right back

INTERNATIONAL: England U20

SIGNED FROM: West Bromwich Albion

PREVIOUS CLUBS: Crewe Alexandra and Preston North End

DID YOU KNOW: Billy was only 16 when he made his league debut for Crewe. His one goal for West Brom was scored against Newcastle United?

14

BORN: Barcelona

POSITION: Midfield

INTERNATIONAL: Spain U17

SIGNED FROM: Wigan Athletic

PREVIOUS CLUBS: Barcelona, Espanyol, Swansea City (loan)

DID YOU KNOW: Jordi played in the same Barcelona youth team as Lionel Messi. Gomez played over 50 times for Barcelona at 'B' level and once in the Spanish Cup, The Copa Del Rey, for the first team. Jordi is seen here with Lionel Messi when they played together at Barcelona?

Jordi GOMEZ

THE NEW BOYS

THE GREAT

Ki's goal in the 4-1 win at Fulham was the 7000th league goal Sunderland had scored in their history.

The Barclays Premier League is the place to be. It's the most exciting league in the world and is watched by people in over 200 countries. With six games to go last season hardly anyone gave Sunderland much chance of staying in it! The Lads were seven points away from safety and three of those six games were away to Manchester City, Chelsea and Manchester United. According to head coach Gus Poyet a miracle was needed – especially as the previous five games had been lost and only one draw had been taken from the four matches before that.

Somehow Sunderland did it. Amazingly they did so with a game to spare - being safe before the final fixture. They did it in style. Starting with a draw at eventual champions Manchester City, where only a late City equaliser prevented victory, Jose Mourinho's 78 match unbeaten home Barclays Premier League record was ended with a stunning 2-1 victory at the Champions League semi finalists while defending champions Manchester United were beaten 1-0. It could have been more - Sunderland struck the Old Trafford woodwork twice.

The revival was seen on Wearside too. Going into the Cardiff game at the end of April maximum points had been taken only three times all season at the Stadium of Light, but Cardiff were crushed 4-0 while following the victory at Old Trafford, West Brom were beaten 2-0 as Sunderland sensationally completed 'The Greatest Escape.'

It was the climax to an astonishing campaign that had seen Sunderland be bottom of the table for the best part of six months but do the double over Newcastle, take four points off champions Manchester City, knock Chelsea and Manchester United out of the Capital One Cup and Southampton out of both cups, as the final of the Capital One Cup and the quarter final of the FA Cup were reached.

It was a season that began disastrously with head coach Paolo Di Canio sacked after taking one point from five games that ended with an awful display at West Brom - the club who the Greatest Escape would be completed against; oddly enough in a game re-arranged because Sunderland had been playing in a cup final on the day The Baggies were originally due to be at the Stadium of Light.

Being a Sunderland supporter is never dull but you will have to live a long time to see another season quite as incredible the one you lived through in 2013-14.

PLAYER OF THE YEAR

Player of the Year Vito Mannone didn't play in the Barclays Premier League until November. Injury to goalkeeper Keiren Westwood gave Mannone a chance he grabbed with both hands. Within a couple of minutes of him coming off the bench Vito saw Sunderland have two players sent off before half time but he remained unbeaten despite playing half the game with his team two men short.

The Italian went on to keep 11 full clean sheets but it was his saves in the Capital One Cup semi final penalty shoot-out at Manchester United that made him a hero.

If a goalkeeper makes a mistake it nearly always results in a goal but even when Mannone failed to hold a late shot from his old Arsenal teammate Samir Nasir that caused a late equaliser at Manchester City, Vito showed his character and after being beaten 12 minutes into his next game at Chelsea didn't concede again until after Sunderland were safe - a run of 355 minutes without conceding.

Sunderland scored all seven penalties awarded to them in the season, but only scored two out of five in the Capital One Cup semi final shoot-out at Manchester United - thankfully that was enough to win!

THE GREAT

CAPITAL ONE CUP

Sunderland reached the final of a major competition for the first time in 22 years and the final of this competition for the first time in 29 years. They were helped by being drawn at home in every round. In a season where until the final fortnight of the campaign only three matches were won at home in the Barclays Premier League somehow eight games out of eight were won at home in the cups, including five in this competition.

A late fight-back from 0-2 down with just 13 minutes to go produced a 4-2 win over MK Dons before Peterborough were defeated 2-0. In form Southampton were then beaten 2-1 before Chelsea arrived for the quarter final just a fortnight after winning a thrilling league game on Wearside by 4-3. It looked like The Blues would win again until former Chelsea player Borini snatched a late equaliser with a sensational night rounded off when Ki grabbed a winner just when it looked like the tie would have to be settled on penalties.

However penalties would be needed in the semi final. A minute from the end of extra time in the second leg at Old Trafford Sunderland looked to be about to lose on away goals. Former Sunderland loan player Jonny Evans had given United a 1-0 lead on the night after Sunderland had beaten them 2-1 at the Stadium of Light. Sunderland had taken close on 9,000 fans to the game - the highest away support anywhere so far in the season - and they were all behind the goal when United' goalie David De Gea let slip a shot from ex Manchester United player Phil Bardsley. Just when it looked as if The Wearsiders had won, up stepped Hernandez to score in injury time of extra time. The score was 3-3 on aggregate with the away goals level too. Penalties would decide who went to Wembley.

After two spot kicks each United led 1-0 before Marcos Alonso and Ki scored for Sunderland. United would not score again, Vito Mannone saving two and another being missed. Sunderland were in the final. Having beaten Manchester United it was Manchester City who lay in wait at Wembley. The sides had already met in one cup final - City winning the pre-season Barclays Asia Tournament 1-0 in Hong Kong.

Sunderland supporters took over Wembley for the showpiece occasion. Many had made the weekend of it and at half time Sunderland deservedly led through a brilliantly taken early Borini goal. The final though was to turn on two top class goals from City within the space of three minutes at the same stage in the second half as Sunderland had scored in the first. The equaliser came though a spectacular shot from Yaya Toure with Samir Nasri catching one perfectly almost straight after. City added a third in the last minute, Jesus Navas catching Sunderland on the break as they pushed for an equaliser to make the final score 3-1.

Sunderland had lost the game but played very well, giving a scare to the top team in the country. The Red and White army also impressed everyone with their support and sporting reaction. It was a day where everything was enjoyable except for the result but it gave a new generation a taste of what being in a cup final is all about and we can't wait for the next time.

FA CUP

Having been starved of exciting cup runs Sunderland supporters had not one but two to enjoy in 2013-14. As well as the thrilling run to the Capital One Cup final the Black Cats also reached the quarter final of the FA Cup.

As in the Capital One Cup Sunderland were blessed with home draws. Carlisle were beaten 3-1 and Conference side Kidderminster defeated 1-0 before Sunderland were presented with top flight opposition in the shape of Southampton in the fifth round. The Saints had their cup hopes in both competitions ended at Sunderland although had England centre forward Rickie Lambert not missed a late sitter Sunderland would have been faced with a replay on the south coast. As it was the lads were drawn to play away from home for the first time, the quarter-final pairing them with former manager Steve Bruce's Hull City. Goalkeeper Oscar Ustari saved a first half penalty but three goals in eight costly second half minutes saw Sunderland's cup ambitions ended just a week after the Capital One Cup final.

16 goals were scored by Sunderland substitutes – the highest number of goals Sunderland have ever had from players who have come off the bench.

BARCLAYS PLAYER OF THE MONTH - JANUARY

Adam Johnson had scored against Spurs in early December but had failed to start any of the month's following four Barclays Premier League fixtures. He spent New Year's Day on the bench until the closing stages against Aston Villa **but ended it as the country's Player of the Month having scored six goals including becoming the only Englishman to score a Barclays Premier League hat trick all season** - at Fulham where he also claimed an assist. A crucial winner at home to Stoke ended the month in which he'd also helped Sunderland to reach Wembley. Johnson continued his purple patch with a goal in the win at Newcastle on February 1st.

BARCLAYS PLAYER OF THE MONTH - APRIL

Connor Wickham was Sunderland's 'Miracle Man'.

Gus Poyet had said Sunderland needed someone to produce the sort of magic Adam Johnson had done in January and Wickham duly delivered. Out on loan for much of the season Wickham had only scored one top-flight goal in his career until he suddenly bagged two in 10 minutes at Manchester City. He added another in the next game at Chelsea and then netted twice and won a penalty against Cardiff. Suddenly the player who had turned 21 on the last day of March had come of age.

Connor Wickham's second goal in the 4-0 win over Cardiff City was the 500th Premier League goal ever scored by Sunderland.

YOUNG PLAYER OF THE YEAR

Fabio Borini turned 23 at the end of March, just three days after he'd had to sit out the away game at Liverpool, who he was on a season long loan from. The Italian international was a huge success finishing the season as joint top scorer with 10 goals that included some of the most important strikes of the season.

The first of Fab's goals was the Goal of the Season, a stunning late screamer to win the derby at home to Newcastle. Three months later he'd score the opening goal in the away win over The Magpies - just one of four pressure penalties Borini coolly slotted away. At Wembley Fabio gloriously put Sunderland ahead in the Capital One Cup final and his top class volley against West Brom ultimately proved to be the goal that put the seal on safety.

THE GREAT

DOUBLE FUN

No matter where the clubs are in the league table derby games against Newcastle United are always of the utmost importance. In the 'Hotbed of Soccer' that is the north-east coming out on top against your local rivals is very important.

2013-14 saw Sunderland win both games against Newcastle in the same season for the first time since 1966-67.

Following on from the win at Newcastle in the previous meeting, doing the double over the Magpies also meant that Sunderland had beaten Newcastle three times in a row for the first time since 1923!

OOH BALLY BALLY

Kevin Ball is a Sunderland legend. In his playing days Bally was one of the finest captains ever because of the way he led by example and got every last drop out of effort out of his teammates. Kevin was asked to step in as caretaker manager after the bad start to the season. He got the players together and fighting for every ball as a unit. Bally's first match in charge saw Sunderland win well in the Capital One Cup against Peterborough who were in great form at the time. He then had two Barclays Premier League games in charge against Liverpool and Manchester United. Both were lost but only after encouraging performances full of fight, which gave everyone hope for the future.

Sunderland scored seven own goals during the season and had players sent off seven times – though one of those was later rescinded (cancelled).

ST ESCAPE

POYETRY IN MOTION

Head coach Gus Poyet took over in October. He quickly showed that he wanted his team to play passing football. Poyet's belief is in keeping the ball. He asked players to change their style, to have belief in themselves and to play attractive football. He was proved right as Sunderland played their way to the Capital One Cup final and out of trouble despite being bottom of the table with just a single point when he took over.

NOT ALL GOOD

Really this was a bad season with a lot of highs. There were some truly fantastic games but also a lot of very disappointing ones. In some Sunderland were just unlucky - such as when Jozy Altidore powered his way through the Arsenal defence at the Stadium of Light and found the back of the net only for the referee to decide to award Sunderland a free kick on the edge of the box - in some they caused their own problems by having men sent off or scoring own goals and in some they just played poorly, sometimes very poorly.

The games against eventually relegated Norwich were especially disappointing: a dull goalless draw at home on the Saturday before Christmas and a dismal 2-0 defeat at Carrow Road in March. The games against Hull - another team who finished below Sunderland - were bad days: two league defeats without scoring with a total of three men sent off (all in the first half) and a tame exit in the FA Cup quarter final, again without scoring.

Early season away defeats at Crystal Palace and West Brom were very poor - the Palace game starting a run of six successive defeats with an average of three goals a game conceded. With 20 Barclays Premier League defeats compared to 10 wins the season undoubtedly had more bad days than good ones, but there were enough good days to keep Sunderland up and some of those good days were very very good indeed.

HIGH FIVE

Sunderland had some brilliant results throughout the season such as the wins over Newcastle, beating eventual champions Manchester City at home and giving Everton their only home defeat in all of 2013 - as well as all the great cup results. **However it was the 'High Five' run towards the end of the season that saved Sunderland.**

Starting with a draw away to Manchester City (who needed a late equaliser to stop Sunderland winning), Sunderland then went to Chelsea and beat them at Stamford Bridge for their first home defeat in 78 league games under Jose Mourinho. A week later the biggest win of the season was recorded as Cardiff were walloped 4-0 before Sunderland won a game at Manchester United for the first time since 1968. With two games to go Sunderland needed just one more win and got it at the first time of asking as West Brom were beaten 2-0.

It was a fourth win in a row following that superb draw at Manchester City. Sunderland had stunned the country and perhaps even themselves. Some said it was a miracle but for others it was the perfect lesson in why you should never, ever give up.

If you have any 3D glasses try using them to look at this picture.

CONNOR WICKHAM

10

29

Valentin ROBERGE

BORN: June 9th 1987, Montreuil, France.

POSITION: Centre back

SIGNED FROM: Maritimo

SUNDERLAND DEBUT: August 17th 2013 Sunderland 0-1 Fulham, Barclays Premier League.

DID YOU KNOW: Roberge is spending the season on loan to Stade de Reims in France.

Youngsters Mikael Mandron, Martin Smith, Duncan Watmore, Joel Dixon and Liam Agnew all have first team squad numbers and are featured in the Under 21 team profiles beginning on page 34.

19

Danny GRAHAM

BORN: June 9th 1987, Gateshead.

POSITION: Centre forward   **SIGNED FROM:** Swansea City

SUNDERLAND DEBUT: January 12th 2012 Sunderland 3-0 West Ham United, Barclays Premier League.

DID YOU KNOW: Danny has over 100 senior league goals to his name.

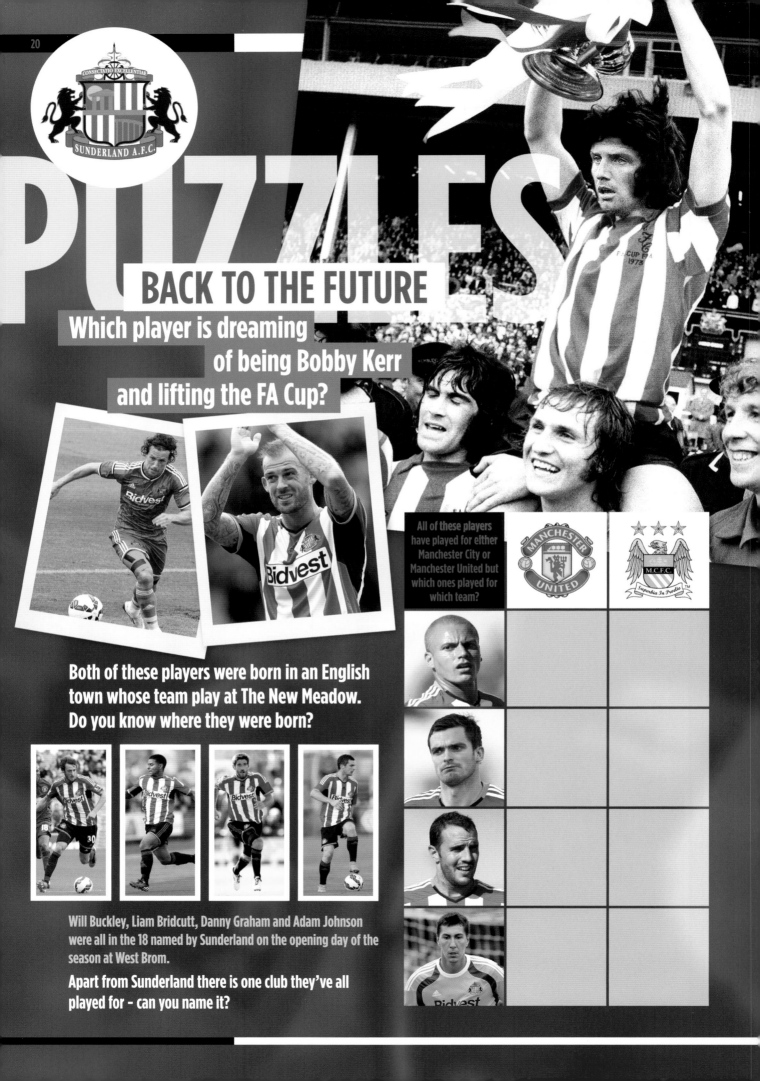

PUZZLES

BACK TO THE FUTURE

Which player is dreaming of being Bobby Kerr and lifting the FA Cup?

Both of these players were born in an English town whose team play at The New Meadow. Do you know where they were born?

Will Buckley, Liam Bridcutt, Danny Graham and Adam Johnson were all in the 18 named by Sunderland on the opening day of the season at West Brom.

Apart from Sunderland there is one club they've all played for – can you name it?

All of these players have played for either Manchester City or Manchester United but which ones played for which team?

FACE OFF

Can you identify these nine Black Cats Stars?

A

B

C

D

E

F

G

H

I

FIRST TEAM SQUAD

Wes BROWN

5

BORN: October 13th 1979, Manchester.

POSITION: Centre back   **INTERNATIONAL:** England

SIGNED FROM: Manchester United

SUNDERLAND DEBUT: August 13th 2011 Liverpool 1-1 Sunderland, Barclays Premier League.

DID YOU KNOW: Wes scored at Wembley for England, against the Czech Republic in 2008?

Seb LARSSON

7

BORN: June 6th 1985, Eskilstuna, Sweden

POSITION: Midfield   **INTERNATIONAL:** Sweden

SIGNED FROM: Birmingham City

SUNDERLAND DEBUT: August 13th 2011, Liverpool 1-1 Sunderland, Barclays Premier League, scored.

DID YOU KNOW: Clubs from England, Germany, Italy and Turkey were all interested in signing Seb before he signed a new contract with Sunderland in the summer?

John O'SHEA

16

BORN: April 30th 1981, Waterford

POSITION: Centre-back   **INTERNATIONAL:** Republic of Ireland

SIGNED FROM: Manchester United

SUNDERLAND DEBUT: August 27th 2011, Swansea City 0-0 Sunderland, Barclays Premier League

DID YOU KNOW: John became the first player from outside Great Britain to captain Sunderland in a cup final when he was skipper in last season's Capital One Cup final?

Steven FLETCHER

9

BORN: March 26th 1987, Shrewsbury   **POSITION:** Striker

INTERNATIONAL: Scotland   **SIGNED FROM:** Wolves

SUNDERLAND DEBUT: August 28th 2012, Sunderland 2-0 Morecambe, Capital One Cup second round.

DID YOU KNOW: Steven Fletcher's middle name is Kenneth. He's named after his father and qualifies for Scotland through his mother?

Adam JOHNSON

11

BORN: July 14th 1987, Sunderland   **POSITION:** Winger

INTERNATIONAL: England   **SIGNED FROM:** Manchester City

SUNDERLAND DEBUT: August 28th 2012, Sunderland 2-0 Morecambe, Capital One Cup second round.

DID YOU KNOW: Adam was the Barclays Premier League Player of the Month in January 2014?

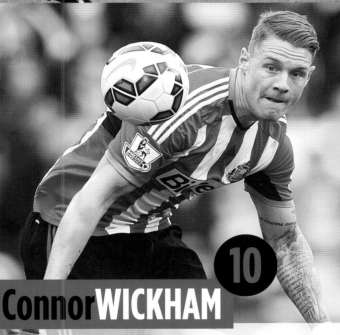

Connor WICKHAM

10

BORN: March 31st 1993, Hereford.

POSITION: Striker   **INTERNATIONAL:** England U21

SIGNED FROM: Ipswich Town

SUNDERLAND DEBUT: August 20th 2011, Sunderland 0-1 Newcastle United, Barclays Premier League, played as a substitute.

DID YOU KNOW: Connor was the Barclays Premier League Player of the Month in April 2014?

Jozy ALTIDORE

17

BORN: November 6th 1989   **POSITION:** Striker

INTERNATIONAL: USA   **SIGNED FROM:** AZ Alkmaar

SUNDERLAND DEBUT: August 17th 2014, Sunderland 0-1 Fulham, Barclays Premier League.

DID YOU KNOW: Jozy has played for clubs in America, Spain, Turkey and the Netherland as well as in England?

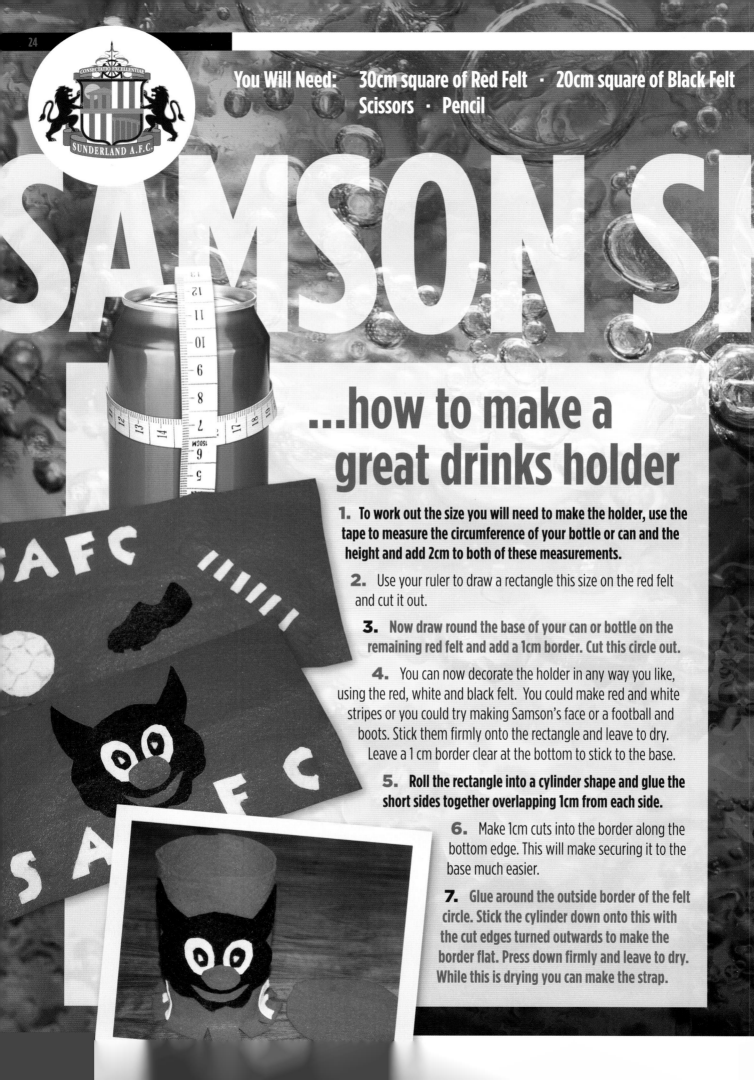

You Will Need: 30cm square of Red Felt · 20cm square of Black Felt
Scissors · Pencil

SAMSON S...

...how to make a great drinks holder

1. To work out the size you will need to make the holder, use the tape to measure the circumference of your bottle or can and the height and add 2cm to both of these measurements.

2. Use your ruler to draw a rectangle this size on the red felt and cut it out.

3. Now draw round the base of your can or bottle on the remaining red felt and add a 1cm border. Cut this circle out.

4. You can now decorate the holder in any way you like, using the red, white and black felt. You could make red and white stripes or you could try making Samson's face or a football and boots. Stick them firmly onto the rectangle and leave to dry. Leave a 1 cm border clear at the bottom to stick to the base.

5. Roll the rectangle into a cylinder shape and glue the short sides together overlapping 1cm from each side.

6. Make 1cm cuts into the border along the bottom edge. This will make securing it to the base much easier.

7. Glue around the outside border of the felt circle. Stick the cylinder down onto this with the cut edges turned outwards to make the border flat. Press down firmly and leave to dry. While this is drying you can make the strap.

20cm square of White Felt · Tape measure and ruler · PVA or fabric glue
Drinks bottle or can – to use for measurements

OWS YOU

8. Measure the length from your waist to the top of your shoulder and down your back to your waist again. Add 5cm to this measurement.

9. Cut strips of the remaining felt to this length and make each one 2.5 cm wide. Now join them together with glue to make one long piece.

10. Stick to the inside of your drinks holder making sure 1.5cm is secured on each end.

Leave to dry overnight.

You now have a great drinks holder to take to the match.

FIRST TEAM SQUAD

Vito **MANNONE** 25

BORN: March 2nd 1988   **POSITION:** Goalkeeper

SIGNED FROM: Arsenal

SUNDERLAND DEBUT: Sunderland 4-2 MK Dons, Capital One Cup 2nd round, August 27th 2013.

DID YOU KNOW: Becoming the hero in the semi final shoot-out at Manchester United meant that Vito spent his birthday playing at Wembley in last season's Capital One Cup final?

El Hadji **BA** 22

BORN: March 5th 1993, Paris

POSITION: Midfield   **INTERNATIONAL:** France U20

SIGNED FROM: Le Havre

SUNDERLAND DEBUT: January 5th 2014, Sunderland 3-1 Carlisle Utd, FA Cup 3rd round.

DID YOU KNOW: El Hadji is on loan to Bastia in France this season?

23 Emanuele **GIACCHERINI**

BORN: May 5th 1985   **POSITION:** Midfield

INTERNATIONAL: Italy   **SIGNED FROM:** Juventus

SUNDERLAND DEBUT: August 17th 2014, Sunderland 0-1 Fulham, Barclays Premier League.

DID YOU KNOW: Emanuele's birthday of May 5th is the anniversary of Sunderland's famous FA Cup final win of 1973?

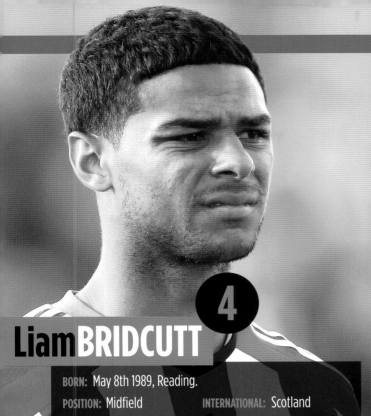

Liam BRIDCUTT

4

BORN: May 8th 1989, Reading.

POSITION: Midfield **INTERNATIONAL:** Scotland

SIGNED FROM: Brighton & Hove Albion

SUNDERLAND DEBUT: February 1st 2014, Newcastle Utd 0-3 Sunderland, Barclays Premier League.

DID YOU KNOW: Liam played for Liverpool boss Brendan Rodgers when he was on loan at Watford in 2008-09?

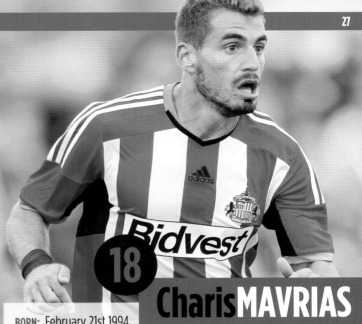

Charis MAVRIAS

18

BORN: February 21st 1994

POSITION: Winger **INTERNATIONAL:** Greece

SIGNED FROM: Panathinaikos

SUNDERLAND DEBUT: Sunderland 4-2 MK Dons, Capital One Cup 2nd round, August 27th 2013.

DID YOU KNOW: When he debuted for former European Cup finalists Panathinaikos in the Champions League in October 2010 Mavrias became the second youngest player to play in the Champions League?

Lee CATTERMOLE

6

BORN: March 21st 1988, Stockton **POSITION:** Midfield

INTERNATIONAL: England U21 **SIGNED FROM:** Wigan Athletic

SUNDERLAND DEBUT: Bolton Wanderers 0-1 Sunderland, Barclays Premier League, 15 August 2009

DID YOU KNOW: Lee played in the final of the UEFA Cup (Now Europa League) for Middlesbrough?

Jordan PICKFORD

13

BORN: March 7th 1994, Washington **POSITION:** Goalkeeper

INTERNATIONAL: England U19 **SIGNED FROM:** SAFC Academy

SUNDERLAND DEBUT: Jordan started this season hoping to make his Sunderland debut.

DID YOU KNOW: Jordan is on loan to Bradford City this season?

Sunderland's nickname is The Black Cats.

Can you match up these nicknames with other teams in the Barclays Premier League?

NICKNAMES: The Magpies, The Hammers, The Saints, The Foxes, The Gunners, The Potters, The Red Devils, The Toffees, The Swans, The Tigers.

TEAMS: Everton, Southampton, Newcastle United, Swansea City, Stoke City, West Ham United, Hull City, Leicester City, Arsenal, Manchester United.

FIND THE ANSWERS ON PAGE 62

A. CLUB: _____ NICKNAME: _____

C. CLUB: _____ NICKNAME: _____

NICKNAME

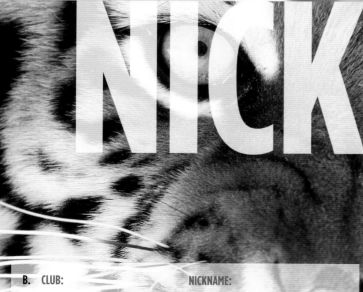

B. CLUB: _____ NICKNAME: _____

D. CLUB: _____ NICKNAME: _____

E. CLUB: NICKNAME:

H. CLUB: NICKNAME:

F. CLUB: NICKNAME:

I. CLUB: NICKNAME:

THAT CLUB

G. CLUB: NICKNAME:

J. CLUB: NICKNAME:

Sunderland supporters jumped aboard the 'Gus-bus' for an amazing ride when Gustavo Augusto Poyet Dominguez took charge of Sunderland last season.

Gus guided the team to Wembley in the Capital One Cup final, sensationally steered Sunderland to safety in the Barclays Premier League and just for good measure reached the FA Cup quarter-final as well.

So who is Gus Poyet and what had happened to him in his career before he joined Sunderland?

ALL ABOARD THE GUS

POYET THE PLAYER

Won the European Cup Winners' Cup in 1995 with Real Zaragoza, beating Arsenal in the final.

Won the Spanish Cup - the Copa del Rey - with Real Zaragoza in 1995.

Moved into English football in the summer of 1997 signing for Chelsea. An attacking midfielder Poyet scored four goals in his first nine games.

Won the European Cup Winners' Cup in 1998 with Chelsea who beat Stuttgart of Germany in the final. Poyet had scored in the semi final against Vicenza of Italy.

Scored one of the most spectacular goals of his career against Sunderland at Chelsea on Sunderland's first match after winning promotion in 1999.

Scored for Chelsea at the Stadium of Light later the same season on a day when Sunderland turned on the style.

Won the FA Cup with Chelsea in 2000, beating Aston Villa in the final.

Gus had scored both goals in the FA Cup semi final ...against Newcastle United who he enjoyed a career long habit of doing very well against.

Signed for Spurs in May 2001 at the age of 33.

Played in the 2002 League Cup final for Spurs alongside Mauricio Taricco who is now his assistant at Sunderland.

Played 25 times for Uruguay with whom he won the South American championship - the Copa America - in 1995, one of three trophies Gus won that year.

Voted best player in his position in the 1995 Copa America.

Gus POYET

TITLE: Head coach

BORN: November 15th 1967, Montevideo, Uruguay

CLUBS AS A PLAYER: Grenoble (France), River Plate (Uruguay), Real Zaragoza (Spain), Chelsea & Tottenham Hotspur.

CLUBS AS A COACH: Swindon Town (Assistant), Leeds United (Assistant), Tottenham Hotspur (First team coach) Brighton and Hove Albion (Manager)

POYET THE MANAGER / COACH

League One Manager of the Year in his first full season at Brighton.

Won promotion to the Championship with Brighton who he then led to the Championship Play offs.

Manager of Brighton when they moved from the Withdean Stadium to their brand new AMEX Stadium.

Manager of Brighton when they knocked Sunderland out of the Capital One Cup in 2011.

Won League Cup as first team coach at Spurs, beating former club Chelsea.

Took Sunderland to a major cup final in his first season when he also miraculously led Sunderland to safety.

Signed a new contract with Sunderland in the summer of 2014.

BUSY!

SPORTING DIRECTOR Lee**CONGERTON**

Gus Poyet has an enormous amount to do. He has to train the players with his coaching staff. He has to plan the tactics, pick the team and deal with the media. Every time you see him interviewed means he's been spending time talking to reporters so that Sunderland supporters know what's going on. Gus needs a bit of help when it comes to signing new players so a very important person at the football club is Lee Congerton.

Lee Congerton is SAFC's Sporting Director. He leads a team of scouting staff who are always on the look out for new players of all ages.

As a player Lee was a youth international for Wales. He played for non league teams Rhyl, Colwyn Bay and Weymouth as well as playing in the league for Crewe Alexandra.

Congerton's career suffered through injuries and he quickly moved into coaching. He worked as a coach with Wrexham and Liverpool as well as with the Wales youth sides. In 2005 Lee moved to Chelsea where Jose Mourinho made him youth team coach. Later, Lee became Chelsea's Chief Scout. He worked with some great young players including Daniel Sturridge and Fabio Borini.

In 2011 Lee moved into German football as Technical Director at Hamburg which was a valuable new experience for him. Lee returned to British football in March 2014 with Sunderland.

Hopefully this season Sunderland won't be fighting against relegation and instead will be in a much better position in the Barclays Premier League table. If you remember last season though you'll know that Sunderland left it late to sensationally climb away from the bottom of the league. As the team fought for the points they needed to make sure they were still playing top flight football this season the players kept talking about 'getting over the line.' They meant getting enough points to be certain of staying up - it's like getting over the line in a race. Try this board game and see if you can…

GET OVER

You'll need a different coloured counter for every player and a dice.

You have to roll a six to start and the winner is the first person to 'Get over the line.'

To make sure it's a fair start, everyone playing should roll the dice first and the person with the highest score should start, the person with the second highest score should go second, and so on. If two people get the same score in the starting roll of the dice they should roll again until one has a higher score.

Once you start you have to tackle every opponent. Whatever number you are on, when you come to an opponent you have to take them on. For instance there is an opponent on square eight. If you are on square five and roll a four, five or six you can only go as far as your next opponent on square eight. This applies to every opponent on the board so if you roll a six when you are on square 20 and can only go as far as your next opponent on square 22 that's just tough. You have to stop at the opponent and then succeed in the task. We warned you it was hard. Have you got what it takes to "Get over the line"?

1

13

2

12

14

3

11

15 You are 2-0 down in a game with Stoke City. Roll your dice twice. You have to get at least one five to move on next time.

4

10

16

5

9

17

6

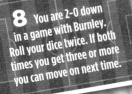
8 You are 2-0 down in a game with Burnley. Roll your dice twice. If both times you get three or more you can move on next time.

18

7

19

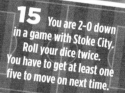

IT'S A HARD GAME TO
WIN AND YOU'LL NEED
TO BE DETERMINED TO
OVERCOME SETBACKS
AND NEVER GIVE UP.

THE LINE...

26

25

27 You are 3-0 down in a game with Manchester City. Roll your dice twice. You have to get a combined total of 10 or more to move on next time.

37 You are 2-0 up in a game with Chelsea. You have to roll your dice more than once. The first roll tells you how many minutes are left in the game and you have to then roll the dice as many times as the first number you get (eg. if the first time is a five you have to roll it five more times). If on any of your rolls after your first roll you get a three you lose and have to try again next time. If you don't get a three you can move on next time and try and get 'over the line.'

24

28

36

38

23

29

35

22 You are 3-0 down in a game with Liverpool. Roll your dice twice. You have to get a combined total of nine or more to move on next time.

30

34

21

31

33

20

32

u21s

LiamAgnew

42

Highly promising midfielder who attended Farringdon School which also produced England international and SAFC Academy player Jordan Henderson. Aggers impressed so much last season he ended the campaign training regularly with the first team and was named on the bench for the first time in the Barclays Premier League in April's exciting draw at Manchester City after excelling on a loan to Boston.

TomBeadling

Commanding centre back who reads the game well and is determined in the challenge. Part of the same year group as midfielder Martin Smith at St. Aidan's School in Sunderland, 'Beado' was born in Barrow but emigrated to Australia when he was 12. He represented Australia at U13 level but returned to the UK a year later and has been part of the SAFC Academy since he was 14.

PeterBurke

Republic of Ireland youth international goalkeeper who like all the young 'keepers at the club works extensively with Academy goalkeeping coach Mark Prudhoe. Hailing from Donegal, Peter is capable of stunning reflex saves.

AndrewCartwright

Andrew has a fine understanding of the game as befits the son of a former professional footballer, his dad Peter played for Newcastle. Whenever you watch him 'Carty' can be heard as well as seen as he is very vocal on the pitch and his appreciation of the tactical side of the game can be seen by his versatility. He most often plays at right back or in midfield but sometimes is used as a support striker.

Joel Dixon

Named as a substitute when Sunderland played Manchester United at the Stadium of Light in the first leg of the 2014 Capital One Cup semi final, Joel is a promising goalkeeper who has spent time on loan with Hartlepool, Leeds and especially Workington. With Sunderland since he was 14, Dixon's distribution is a strength of his game.

David Ferguson

Centre back or left back who was a Sunderland season ticket holder as a youngster. David began his career with Darlington making six first team appearances for The Quakers and appeared in the first pre-season friendly of the 2014-15 season against his old club, now called Darlington 1883. He was named as a substitute in the Barclays Premier League game away to Tottenham Hotspur at the end of the 2012-13 campaign.

Scott Harrison

Born in Middlesbrough in 1993, strong centre back Scott started in 'Boro's Development Centre and played senior football for Darlington before joining Sunderland in 2012. He gained Football League experience on loan to Bury and Hartlepool last season having been an unused sub for Sunderland at Spurs on the last day of the season before last. He re-joined Hartlepool on loan again at the start of this season.

Lynden Gooch

Coming from Santa Cruz in California, Lynden is a regular cross Atlantic traveller as a member of the USA U20 squad. In July 2014 he helped his country to top their group in an invitational tournament. The woodwork denied striker Lynden three times in a goalless draw with Australia that stopped the States having a 100% record after beating Chile and Bermuda.

George Honeyman

A well balanced, nimble, creative midfielder who started Sunderland's first pre-season game of the season against Darlington 1883. Hailing from Prudhoe, George has been developing his game at Sunderland's Academy from the age of 11.

U21s

Carl Lawson

Sunderland born forward who can play as a striker or behind the target-man but is especially dangerous when cutting in from the left as his well timed runs can be difficult to pick up. Carl has been with the club since he was 12 having been discovered playing in the Russell Forster League.

Tom McNamee

A strong and dominant defender in a traditional centre-half style, Tommy has developed his game so that he looks to retain possession well. A fierce competitor, Tommy comes from Shotley Bridge and has been at Sunderland since U14 level.

Connor Oliver

Made his Football League full debut with a 'Man of the Match' performance for Hartlepool at Plymouth in April 2014 having appeared briefly as a sub the previous week. Connor has an imposing physical presence which he can use to good effect in midfield or defence. He also has a good range of vision, likes to switch play with a diagonal pass and has developed the ability to run with the ball along with knowing when to do so.

38

Mikael Mandron

French born striker who made two substitute appearances for Sunderland first team the season before last and added more experience on loan to Fleetwood Town last season, scoring his first senior goal against York. Scored 10 goals for the U21s last season including a hat trick away to Arsenal.

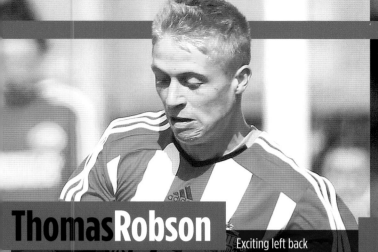

Thomas**Robson**

Exciting left back who loves to get forward and can play on the wing, Tommy is one of several youngsters on Sunderland's books who hail from the Shotley Bridge area and also one of a small group who number Darlington amongst their previous clubs.

Martin**Smith**

Martin is another of Sunderland's youth squad who grew up as a dedicated Sunderland supporter. A central midfielder with plenty in his locker, Smithy can tackle, pass, likes a shot and is always keen to take a penalty.

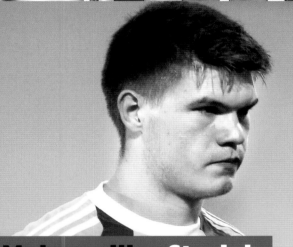

Maksymilian**Stryjek**

Poland U18 international goalkeeper 'Max' is sometimes known as 'the monster' because he looks so big and dominant in goal. Capable of some incredible reflex saves, he has previously played for MKS Polonia.

Duncan**Watmore**

An exciting right sided forward who is also studying for a Business and Economics degree at Newcastle University. Signed in May 2013 from Altrincham where he had impressed with 15 goals, several of them spectacular ones. Manchester born, he was with Manchester United from the age of six to 12. Watmore is now blossoming into a forward to keep an eye on. He loves to run at people and cause problems. Gained experience on loan to Hibs in Scotland last season.

Jassem**Sukar**

Hartlepool lad Jass Sukar is a left sided defender who can play in central defence or at full back. His progress was interrupted by injury last season and he is looking to consistently demonstrate what he is capable of this season.

Sunderland Ladies have enjoyed their first season as members of the FA Women's Super League. Why not go and see their often highly entertaining matches at the Eppleton CW ground in Hetton?

Lead by head coach Claire Robinson and team manager Mick Mulhern, the Ladies have a hard working team supporting them. General manager Sonia Kulkarni oversees everything while additional coaching staff include: assistant coach Melanie Reay, goalkeeping coach Anthony Forrester and Julie Twaddle the strength and conditioning coach, all backed up by physio Sophie Marr. Here is an introduction to the Sunderland Ladies squad from their first season in the FAWSL.

GOALKEEPERS

Helen Alderson: Born in 1989 Helen was part of the England squad who played in the 2008 FIFA Women's U20 World Cup in Chile

Rachael Laws: A winner of the Northern Premier League with Sunderland and the FA Women's Super League with Liverpool who she has represented on loan.

DEFENDERS

Stephanie Bannon: SAFC Ladies captain who has been inspirational in leading the team to three successive league winning seasons.

Megan Beer: Doubles as a coach when working with players at the Women's Football Academy including some of her own Gateshead College teammates.

Victoria Greenwell: Dead ball specialist who scored free kicks in the first two games of the season. Chosen for GB at the World University Games in China.

Abby Holmes: There to stop goals but grabbed the headlines with a last minute winner against Millwall to clinch the Premier League title two seasons ago.

Gemma Wilson: Sunderland Ladies longest serving player, the experience of hard tackling Gemma is invaluable to the squad.

MIDFIELDERS

Rebekah Bass: Rebekah turned 20 in 2014, has captained the England Colleges team and been selected by England at U20 level.

Lauren Briggs: Teenager capable of overcoming hurdles as a footballer or as a horsewoman, horses being her other passion.

Rachel Furness: Northern Ireland international who once scored a hat-trick against Croatia and joined her international and club colleague Sarah McFadden in being selected to represent Great Britain in China in the World University Games.

Natalie Gutteridge: Scored at the Stadium of Light in 2009, a goal that took Sunderland into the 2009 FA Women's Cup final against Arsenal at Derby. Suffered a bad injury in 2013.

Kelly McDougall: Veteran who has won nine England caps, one of 12 Sunderland players with international experience.

Sarah McFadden: Northern Ireland international who teaches at Gateshead College. One of a quartet of Sunderland players selected for the GB women's team at the World University Games in Shenzhen, China.

Brogan McHugh: A student who played in the 2013 European Championships at U17 level for England.

Hayley Sharp: A new signing in 2014, Hayley travelled to China as part of the GB squad at the World University Games

FORWARDS

Abbey Joice: Teenage forward whose skill on the ball impresses her teammates so much they call her 'Little Messi' - not that Lionel is big! Called up with Beth Mead by England U19s for their European Championship qualifying games in 2014.

Emma Kelly: England U17 international, Emma has captained her country. Not 20 until 2017, Emma has come through the ranks at SAFC and is one for the future.

Beth Mead: A goal machine with a very impressive 59 goals to her name in the last two seasons which propelled her into the England U20 squad for 2014's FIFA Women's U20 World Cup in Canada.

Keira Ramshaw: England U23 star who defenders mess with at their peril... she is a black belt in karate!

Sophie Williams: A winger who looks to spark attacks - during the week she works as an electrician.

The Stadium of Light is one of Wearside's finest landmarks.

SPOT THE

It can be spotted from all around the area and wherever you view the Stadium of Light from it fills Sunderland supporters with the pride that comes from knowing the football club is the heartbeat of a city that is simply football daft.

Although the stadium can be seen from miles around it is something of a Dr. Who style Tardis, in that it is bigger on the inside than the outside.

This is because when the stadium was built the bottom tier of seats and the pitch were constructed below ground level on the site of the old Wearmouth Colliery.

Cleverly this made the stadium cheaper to build as the stands didn't have to be as high as they would have needed to be if the pitch was at ground level. Nonetheless the Stadium of Light still stands proudly on the banks of the River Wear and as you can see from the photographs, it can be seen from lots of vantage points in and around the city.

Every team needs a team behind them and Sunderland's first team coaching staff work together to prepare the players for every game.

If you see the coaching staff in the dug out at the match or on TV do you know who is who?

Here's your guide to head coach Gus Poyet's staff.

Gus Poyet's right hand man comes from Argentina, the South American country which borders Uruguay, where Poyet was born. Nicknamed 'Tano'. Taricco began his career with the same club Sunderland cult hero Julio Arca played for before coming to England, Argentinos Juniors. In Tano's case he moved to Europe in 1994 when he signed for Ipswich Town where he made his name as an attacking, physically strong left back. He was Ipswich's Player of the Year in 1997 and transferred to Tottenham Hotspur in January 1999 for £1.75m after playing 189 times for 'The Tractor Boys'.

It was at White Hart Lane that 'Tano' played alongside Gus Poyet. In five years in the capital the defender played 158 games for Spurs before moving to West Ham where he signed for Alan Pardew who of course later was manager of Newcastle on the day Sunderland won under Poyet for the first time. Oddly enough the South American duo's first game in charge of Brighton was also against Mr. Pardew.

Taricco's time at West Ham was short-lived as he offered to cancel his contract after sustaining a hamstring injury less than half an hour into his debut at Millwall in November 2004. 'Tano' returned to Argentina before deciding to move to Italy where he was persuaded to begin playing again and also began learning to be a coach.

THE TEAM

In 2009 'Tano' teamed up with Gus Poyet at Brighton playing a handful of games for the Seagulls before focussing fully on assisting Poyet on the coaching staff.

Mauricio TARICCO

TITLE: Assistant Head coach

BORN: 10/10/73, Buenos Aires, Argentina.

CLUBS AS A PLAYER: Career: Argentinos Juniors (debut 1993), Ipswich Town (1994-98), Spurs (1999-04) West Ham (2004), A.S. Villasimius (Italy) (2005-09) Brighton (2009-13).

CLUBS AS A COACH: Brighton (2009-13), Sunderland (2013-)

A tough tackling midfielder during his playing days, Charlie Oatway is a larger than life character who makes sure training includes a bit of fun as well as a lot of hard work.

Funnily enough he's not actually called 'Charlie' that's just his nickname as it was said he'd be a 'proper Charlie' after he was named after the entire Queens Park Rangers team who had won promotion in the year he was born!

Charlie OATWAY

TITLE: First team coach

BORN: 28/11/73, Hammersmith

CLUBS AS A PLAYER: Wimbledon age 14-16 (1985-92), Yeading as semi-pro (1993-94), Cardiff City (1994-95), Torquay Utd. (1995-97), Brentford (1997-99), Lincoln City (loan) (1998), Brighton & Hove Albion (1999-2007), Havant & Waterlooville (player & assistant manager) (2007-09),

CLUBS AS A COACH: Havant & Waterlooville, Brighton & Hove Albion

Andy enjoyed a lengthy playing career representing ten clubs including half a dozen loans. Now he works as a specialist goalkeeping coach with all of Sunderland's senior goalkeepers and can always be seen waiting to greet the 'keeper as the teams leave the field.

Andy BEASLEY

TITLE: Goalkeeping coach

BORN: 5/2/64, Sedgely, Staffordshire.

CLUBS AS A PLAYER: Luton (1980-84), Mansfield Town (1984-93), Gillingham (loan 1983-84), Peterborough (loan 1986-87), Scarborough (loan 1987-88), Kettering Town (loan 1988-89), Cheltenham Town (loan 1989-90), Bristol Rovers (Loan 1989-90), Doncaster Rovers (1993-94), Chesterfield (1994-97)

CLUBS AS A COACH: Goalkeeper coach at Nottingham Forest (2004-06), Swindon Town (2006) Leeds, (2006-12), Brighton (2012-13)

BEHIND THE TEAM

Italian Antonio has worked at some of the continent's top clubs. The author of a book about the re-education of a player following a cruciate ligament injury, Pintus has also written several medical papers.

A fitness expert, Antonio is far removed form the stereotype of the fitness fanatic. Like his fellow coaching staff he appreciates the value of enjoyment and is always ready with a smile or a joke.

Antonio PINTUS

TITLE: Fitness coach

BORN: 29/6/62, Torino

CLUBS AS A COACH: ACD Settimo (1986-1991), Juventus (1991-98), Chelsea (1998-2000), Udinese (2001), Monaco (2001-05), Juventus (2006-07), West Ham (2008-10), Olympic Marseille (2010-11), GS Consulat Marseille (2011-12), Palermo (2012-13).

Incredibly for a team at the wrong end of the table for most of the season last year Sunderland impressively averaged over 41,000 with a top attendance of 46,313 for the win over Newcastle United.

However that wasn't the highest number of people to cram into the Stadium of Light as over 52,000 were there to see One Direction at the end of May.

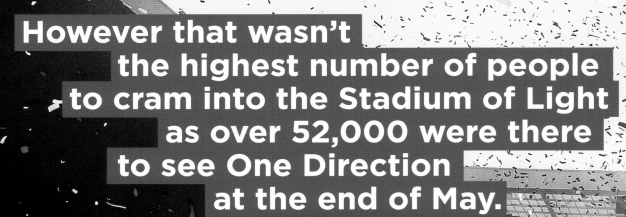

One Direction are the world's biggest boy band and tickets for this major event sold out in superfast time. Not even rainy weather could dampen the spirits of the excited 'Directioneers' on the opening night of 1D's 'Where We Are' tour.

The pop superstars left their audience in no doubt as to where they were with band members Harry and Niall getting the crowd to chant 'Sunderland' and 'Ha'way the Lads.' The fans needed no second invitation to cheer on the boys who had rehearsed at the Stadium of Light on a previous visit when Niall (Horan not Quinn!) even donned a Sunderland strip for a little kick-a-bout which saw him post pictures of himself on Instagram.

Featuring number one singles 'What Makes You Beautiful' and 'Little Things' One Direction climaxed their 22 song set with 'Best Song Ever.' It might not have been the best song ever nor the best gig ever but rest assured if you are a One Direction fan it certainly felt like it on what was another brilliant evening of top class entertainment at the stadium which has made itself the north east's premier venue to the biggest stars in the music business.

Samson
the Cat

Samson's SUMS

Delilah has told Samson to do his sums. You need to know Sunderland's squad numbers to work them out.

Can you help Samson?

1	Costel Pantilimon
2	Billy Jones
3	Patrick van Aanholt
4	Liam Bridcutt
5	Wes Brown
6	Lee Cattermole
7	Seb Larsson
8	Jack Rodwell
9	Steven Fletcher
10	Connor Wickham
11	Adam Johnson
13	Jordan Pickford
14	Jordi Gomez
16	John O'Shea
17	Jozy Altidore
18	Charis Mavrias
19	Danny Graham
23	Emanuele Giaccherini
25	Vito Mannone
27	Santiago Vergini
29	Valentin Roberge
30	Will Buckley
38	Mikael Mandron
40	Martin Smith
41	Duncan Watmore
42	Liam Agnew
48	Joel Dixon

1 BROWN + GOMEZ =

2 FLETCHER + ALTIDORE =

3 JOHNSON + VERGINI =

4 BUCKLEY − MANNONE =

5 GIACCHERINI − MAVRIAS =

6 MANNONE − CATTERMOLE =

7 LARSSON X RODWELL =

8 VERGINI ÷ VAN AANHOLT =

9 MAVRIAS ÷ FLETCHER =

10 O'SHEA + ROBERGE −

PANTILIMON ÷ BRIDCUTT =

How did you get on?

Answers on page 62

UNDER18s

Dan Casey

A commanding centre back who has played for the Republic of Ireland at U15, U16 and U17 level. Liverpool, Celtic, Leicester and Wolves were all interested in Dan before he decided to come to Sunderland.

Avis Ganiyu

Left winger who was called up by the Republic of Ireland U17 squad for a pre-season tournament in Hungary in the summer of 2014 shortly after he joined SAFC. Previously Avis had represented his country at U15 and U16 level. A finely balanced winger with pace Ganiyu is an eye-catching player.

Kieran Graham

Locally born right midfielder who can also play off the front man, Kieran is a nimble player who has been coming to the Academy since he was 7.

Denver Hume

A left back from Northumberland who has been attending the Academy of Light since he was 10.

David Lowrie

Locally born defender who started five games at U18 level in late 2013 as well as appearing in the FA Youth Cup at Ipswich. David has been attending the Sunderland academy since he was nine.

Luke Molyneux

Co. Durham born player who operates on the left of midfield but can also play on the right. All of the other professional north east clubs showed interest in Luke who has been attending the Academy at SAFC since he was 14. Started a game either side of Christmas last year including one against Newcastle.

Andrew Nelson

A direct striker potentially lethal when the ball is played in front of him. Scored on his first start at U18 level against Middlesbrough in November 2013 and added two more on his third appearance in a 7-0 thrashing of Bolton later the same month.

Jean-Yves Poame

Powerful midfielder who likes to get forward. Jean-Yves has represented the Republic of Ireland at U15, U16 and U17 level and has been coming to the Sunderland academy since he was 15.

Greg Purvis

Goalkeeper from Northumberland who started attending the Academy of Light as an U13. Greg has been involved in England training camps.

Daniel Pybus

England youth midfielder whose dad was a professional player for York. Likes to drive forward with the ball and can play as a second striker. An eye-catching presence in the middle of the park, Dan played 15 times at U18 level before leaving school.

Josh Robson

Harrogate born right footed full back who can also play in central defence. As a youngster Josh played for Guide Post, Bedlington and Ponteland United before starting with Sunderland at the U10 age level.

Daniel Wright

Quick off the mark central midfielder who is very mobile and likes to hit sharp passes. A South Shields lad who played for Monkton Athletic before joining Sunderland. Made his U18 debut in August 2013. An England U17 international.

rdan Blinco

Winger who came to prominence playing for Ushaw Moor in Durham. A well balanced player who has a turn of pace and the ability to deliver a telling cross as well as good finishing. 'Blink' was born in Exeter but moved to the north east when he was five and was at Darlington before joining Sunderland at the age of 15.

Ross Colquhoun

Sunderland born centre half who debuted at U18 level in December 2012. Began in the Russell Forster League and played for Lambton Lions and Whiteleas before joining Sunderland when he was 10.

Ryan Ellison

A right back from Stockport who was with Manchester City before signing for Sunderland in the summer of 2013, having first played for the Black Cats in December 2012. Likes to get forward and scored in the opening pre-season friendly of this season.

Rees Greenwood

A right-winger who can be torture for defenders to face. Rees has the ability to take people on and when in full flow can glide past opponents. Began with Winlaton and has been developing at Sunderland since he was eight.

Michael Ledger

A right back or centre half from Consett, Michael always had a Sunderland season ticket when he was growing up. He played his first game for the U18s in October 2012 and hopes to one day fulfil a dream by playing for the first team.

Dylan McEvoy

A product of the famed Wallsend Boys Club, 'Dill' prefers to play centre midfield but can also operate in wide positions. A hard working player, Dylan is good technically and played his first game for Sunderland at U18 level at Liverpool in February 2013.

Ethan Robson

A central midfield player who has great vision and plenty of ability. Joined the Academy at Sunderland when he was eight and made his first appearance for the U18s in April 2012.

James Talbot

Goalkeeper from the Republic of Ireland who was the Player of the Year for his age group in Ireland in 2013 and is an U16 and U17 international. James played against Chelsea, Man United, Middlesbrough and Reading in his first season at SAFC.

Only around three and a half million people live in Uruguay, which is less than half the size of London in terms of people. Around 53 million people live England. Uruguay is the second smallest country in South America.

It can get very windy in Uruguay, which is quite a flat county.

People speak Spanish in Uruguay.

Uruguay is in the southern hemisphere. When it is summer in England it is winter in Uruguay.

The most famous football clubs in Uruguay are called Nacional and Penarol.

Gus Poyet is from a country called Uruguay, which is in South America.
It is a small country
but one with a fantastic football tradition.

HOME

GUS POYET: URUGUAY

URUGUAY

Uruguay became the first ever World Champions when they won the first World Cup in 1930. They had also been champions when winning the gold medal at the two previous Olympic Games in 1924 and 1928.

Uruguay won the World Cup again in 1950 and were semi finalists in 2010. In 2014 they were in England's group.

Around one third of the people who live in Uruguay live in Montevideo, which is 12 times larger than Salta, which is the second biggest city in Uruguay.

Poyet played in Uruguay for a club called River Plate who play in red and white stripes. There is another more famous club called River Plate who play in nearby Argentina.

Luis Suarez, Edinson Cavani, Diego Forlan and Gus Poyet are famous footballers from Uruguay.

Romania is a country on the edge of Central and South-Eastern Europe.

51

It has borders with five countries and the Black Sea. Increasing numbers of people go there for their holidays, usually to seaside resorts or to the Carpathian mountains which are in the centre of the country.

Costel began his career with a team in his home city of Bacau, called Aerostar Bacau.

There are believed to be around 5000 brown bears in Romania.

Goalkeeper Costel Pantilimon played for Manchester City against Sunderland at Wembley in the 2014 Capital One Cup final before signing for Sunderland in the summer.

Bacau is about half the size of Sunderland and is the 15th biggest city in Romania.

Bacau is almost 190 miles north of the capital of Bucharest which is six times bigger than the second biggest city in the country.

COSTEL PANTILIMON: ROMANIA

The most famous team in Romania are Steau Bucharest.

They won the European Cup in 1986, were finalists in 1989 and played at Sunderland in a testimonial for Sunderland player Richard Ord in 1996.

Tennis is also a very popular sport in Romania. Their best ever player was Ilie Nastase who twice reached the final at Wimbledon in the 1970s when he won the U.S. and French Open Championships.

The most famous Romanian footballer of all time is Gheorghe Hagi who was a superstar who played for both Real Madrid and Barcelona.

Nowadays Romania has a new tennis hero, Simona Halep who reached the semi final at Wimbledon and the French final in 2014.

It is one of the most advanced countries in the world but it can get very cold and has snow for much of the year.

SWEDEN

The famous car makers Volvo & Saab come from Sweden.

The furniture maker IKEA is another famous Swedish company.

Sweden is a big country but not many people live there. Most people live in the south of the country. Much of the north of the nation is forests and some of it is within the Arctic Circle.

SPAIN

The capital of Sweden is a beautiful city called Stockholm.

Seb Larsson is one of Sweden's top international players.

SEB LARSSON: SWEDEN

Zlatan Ibrahimovic is Sweden's most famous current player. In November 2012 he scored four goals in one game against England including one of the most spectacular goals you could ever see.

Sweden reached the World Cup final when they were the host nation in 1958. Ice hockey is a very popular sport in the country and Sweden have been world champions at ice hockey eight times.

One of the best tennis players of all time is Bjorn Borg from Sweden.

Pop superstars ABBA come from Sweden.

Have you studied the Vikings at school? Some of the Vikings came from Sweden.

Spain is a very popular place for English people to go on holiday or even to live. Spain has many famous holiday islands including Ibiza, Majorca Menorca and the Canary Islands, which include Tenerife and Lanzerote.

Paella is a very famous dish that comes from Spain where the most famous drink is called Sangria.

One of the world's best tennis players, Rafa Nadal, is from Spain.

Jordi Gomez was born in Barcelona. He began his career with them and played for their first team in the Spanish Cup – the Copa Del Rey.

Jordi also played for Espanyol, the other team in Barcelona – and he played for Spain at U17 level.

Bilbao, Seville and Valencia are some of Spain's other great cities.

JORDI GOMEZ: SPAIN

Spain's capital city is Madrid. In 2014 the Champions League final was between Real Madrid and Atletico Madrid. This was the first time that the final had been played between two clubs from the same city.

Real Madrid won to become the first team to win the European Cup / Champions League 10 times.

The guitar comes from Spain.

Only Italian side AC Milan have been champions of Europe even half as many times as Real Madrid.

Spain have won the last two European Championships. The national team have been European champions three times. Spain won the World Cup for the first time in 2010.

One of the most important parts of a season for a football team is pre-season. That is the time leading up to the start of the first competitive game. **It is the time when a football team gets as fit as possible after the summer break.** It is also when the coaching staff work on getting the team organised to play in the style they want them to.

PRE-SEASON

Have you ever been in a Christmas Nativity play at school? **What did you have to do before the performance?** You had to know what to do and when to do it as well as how to work with everyone else.

It's like that for footballers in pre-season. It's like a rehearsal before the big day of the first performance, which for Sunderland this season was at West Bromwich Albion where they worked hard for a 2-2 draw.

This summer Sunderland played eight friendly games as they warmed up for the first Barclays Premier League game of the season. They kicked off by beating Darlington 1883, Carlisle United and Hartlepool United in away games that featured a lot of young players.

The next stage was to head off to Portugal for just over a week. Guaranteed warm weather training in Portugal meant the squad could concentrate on building up fitness and team play. Having already played three games the coaching staff and players had some things to work on and did so in Portugal where they won one, drew one and lost one of the three games they played. All three were tight affairs with just one goal scored and one goal conceded on the trip. Recreativo de Huelva were beaten 1-0, CD National inflicted a 1-0 defeat before a goalless draw with Vitoria Setubal.

The final stage of pre-season saw two continental clubs come to the north east to meet Sunderland at Bishop Auckland's Heritage Park which had staged the opening friendly against Darlington 1883. First to visit were Spanish side Real Betis who had just dropped out of La Liga, the top league in Spain. Two days later Italian Serie 'A' outfit Udinese arrived for what was Sunderland's final rehearsal.

Both Real Betis and Udinese were beaten 2-0 to give Sunderland a record of six wins a draw and a defeat from the eight pre-season friendlies.

NORTH EAST

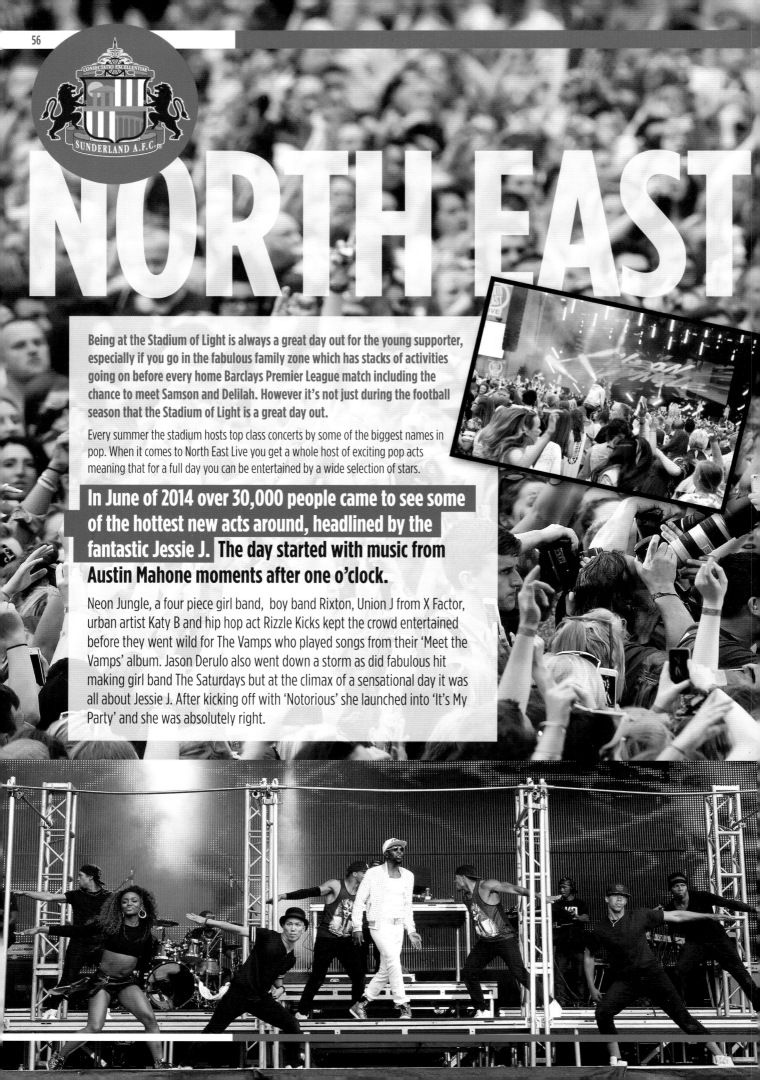

Being at the Stadium of Light is always a great day out for the young supporter, especially if you go in the fabulous family zone which has stacks of activities going on before every home Barclays Premier League match including the chance to meet Samson and Delilah. However it's not just during the football season that the Stadium of Light is a great day out.

Every summer the stadium hosts top class concerts by some of the biggest names in pop. When it comes to North East Live you get a whole host of exciting pop acts meaning that for a full day you can be entertained by a wide selection of stars.

In June of 2014 over 30,000 people came to see some of the hottest new acts around, headlined by the fantastic Jessie J. **The day started with music from Austin Mahone moments after one o'clock.**

Neon Jungle, a four piece girl band, boy band Rixton, Union J from X Factor, urban artist Katy B and hip hop act Rizzle Kicks kept the crowd entertained before they went wild for The Vamps who played songs from their 'Meet the Vamps' album. Jason Derulo also went down a storm as did fabulous hit making girl band The Saturdays but at the climax of a sensational day it was all about Jessie J. After kicking off with 'Notorious' she launched into 'It's My Party' and she was absolutely right.

LIVE

JESSIE J
NORTH EAST
LIVE
STADIUM OF
LIGHT
2014

At every home game supporters get to see how great the Stadium of Light is but most fans have never been to the Academy of Light. Sunderland's training ground is one of the very best in the country, just as the Stadium of Light is one of England's top grounds.

BEHIND THE

THE PLAQUE UNVEILED BY SVEN GORAN ERIKSSON AT THE OPENING OF THE ACADEMY

THE RECEPTION AREA OF THE ACADEMY OF LIGHT

SWIMMING POOLS AT THE ACADEMY

SUNDERLAND'S OWNER AND CHAIRMAN ELLIS SHORT WITH SIR TREVOR BROOKING AT THE OPENING OF THE INDOOR BARN

SCENES AT THE ACADEMY

Attitude is contagious, is yours worth catching?

An open mind accepts what a closed mind rejects

TUNNEL ART LEADING TO MOST OF THE TRAINING PITCHES

THE PITCH USED FOR U21 AND U18 GAMES AT THE ACADEMY OF LIGHT

THE INDOOR TRAINING BARN

AN ALL WEATHER SURFACE

The Academy of Light was opened just over 10 years ago by the then England manager Sven Goran Eriksson. The academy includes a gym, swimming pools and an indoor pitch which enables youngsters to work on the development of their skills.

The Academy of Light provides top class facilities for the first team and all of the club's development players coming through the academy. Players from the age of eight upwards depend upon the amenities of the academy where the staff are dedicated to getting the best out of players whether they are an established senior international or a young lad hoping to become a professional footballer.

Here are 14 questions on 2014.

Give yourself three points
for everyone you get right
and one point for any answer
you get partly correct.

The most points you can get is 42.

40 OR MORE POINTS	YOU ARE THE EXPERT OF EXPERTS
35 TO 39 POINTS	GREAT KNOWLEDGE
30-34 POINTS	YOU KNOW YOUR STUFF
20-29 POINTS	DECENT PERFORMANCE
11-19 POINTS	MID TABLE.
6-10 POINTS	JUST ABOVE THE RELEGATION ZONE.
0-5 POINTS	KEEP READING AND YOU'LL IMPROVE

Who scored Sunderland's first goal of 2014?

Who scored Sunderland's final goal of the 2013-14 season?

Who scored Sunderland's opening goal in this season's
Barclays Premier League?

Which country did Sunderland visit for three pre-season games?

Which two players scored their penalties in the shoot out
that took Sunderland to Wembley in January's Capital One Cup
semi final second leg away to Manchester United?

Who did Sunderland play in the first Capital One Cup game
of this season?

Which two players did Sunderland sign from Brighton
and Hove Albion in 2014?

Which two players did Sunderland sign from Manchester City in 2014?

Which former Barcelona player did Sunderland sign in 2014?

Who scored Sunderland's first goal at the Stadium of Light this season?

Who were the last team to visit the Stadium of Light in the 2013-14 season?

Which non-league team visited the Stadium of Light in the FA Cup in 2014?

Who scored a Barclays Premier League hat trick for Sunderland in January?

Which two Sunderland players won Barclays Premier League Player
of the Month awards in the first half of 2014?

FIND THE ANSWERS ON PAGE 62

EST YOURSELF ON 2014

New Year's Day is scheduled to be the beginning not just of a new year, but also the start of the second half of the season. Sunderland's eagerly anticipated trip to the reigning Barclays Premier League champions Manchester City is scheduled to be the 20th game of the season.

Will Sunderland do better in the last 19 matches of the season than they have in the first 19 games?

There's no reason for The Lads to be daunted by a trip to City. Of course they are a truly brilliant team who can beat the best in the world but Sunderland have a good record against them and will go there aiming to make things difficult for City again. Of course Sunderland met City at Wembley in 2014 in a cup final and cup football comes around early in the new year in the shape of the FA Cup before the first home Barclays Premier League game of 2015, which is against Liverpool. The visit of the men from Anfield will be another really tough fixture and things won't get any easier the following weekend when a trip to Tottenham will again pit Sunderland against a leading side. Depending upon earlier results hopefully there'll then be more cup football before January ends with the visit of Burnley just as the January transfer window is closing.

February brings trips to Swansea City and Manchester Utd with home matches against QPR & WBA in between them before an early March Tuesday night visit to Hull City, almost exactly a year after last season's FA Cup run ended at the same ground. Aston Villa then come to Sunderland before March ends with another trip to London to face West Ham.

Every point counts from the first day of the season but by the time the page for April is turned over on your calendar the battle for final positions in the Barclays Premier League is likely to be so tight that the games become even more exciting. None are likely to be as important as the one scheduled for Saturday April 4th. This is when Sunderland entertain Newcastle United. There are derby games all over the country but in the north east this is the big one and Sunderland will hope to repeat last year's victory over the Magpies at the Stadium of Light.

A week later Sunderland are at home again, this time against The Eagles of Crystal Palace rather than the Magpies of Newcastle before the month ends with away trips to Arsenal and Stoke City.

This season ends later than last year's, when football was preparing for the FIFA World Cup. This time round May begins with Southampton making the long trip to Wearside before the Black Cats travel to Everton. Last season's champions of the Championship, Leicester City provide the opposition for the last home game of the season on May 16th before the curtain is brought down on the Barclays Premier League campaign on Sunday May 24th when Sunderland travel to Chelsea, scene of one of their finest wins of 2014.

Who knows if Sunderland will have a game the following weekend when it is the FA Cup final but one thing is for sure, the second half of the season is something to look forward to.

JANUARY

Thu	1	Manchester City	A	
Sat	3			FA Cup 3
Sat	10	Liverpool	H	
Sat	17	Tottenham Hotspur	A	
Wed	21			COCup Semi (1)
Sat	24			FA Cup 4
Wed	28			COCup Semi (2)
Sat	31	Burnley	H	

FEBRUARY

Sat	7	Swansea City	A	
Tue	10	Queens Park Rangers	H	
Sat	14			FA Cup 5
Sat	21	West Bromwich Albion	H	
Sat	28	Manchester United	A	

MARCH

Sun	1			COCup Final
Tue	3	Hull City	A	
Sat	7			FA Cup 6
Sat	14	Aston Villa	H	
Sat	21	West Ham United	A	

APRIL

Sat	4	Newcastle United	H	
Sat	11	Crystal Palace	H	
Sat	18	Arsenal	A	FA Cup Semi
Sat	25	Stoke City	A	

MAY

Sat	2	Southampton	H	
Sat	9	Everton	A	
Sat	6	Leicester City	H	
Sun	24	Chelsea	A	
Sat	30			FA Cup Final

Fixtures are subject to change. See Sunderland's match programme Red & White or safc.com for up to date information.
Copyright 2014 Football DataCo Ltd.

2ND HALF OF THE SEASON

ANSWERS

PAGE 20: PUZZLES

Back to the Future: Lee Cattermole

New Meadow: Steven Fletcher and Billy Jones were both born in Shrewsbury

One Club: Watford is the club that Will Buckley, Liam Bridcutt, Danny Graham and Adam Johnson have all played for as well as Sunderland.

United or City: John O'Shea and Wes Brown used to play for Manchester United while Costel Pantilimon and Adam Johnson are both former Manchester City players.

PAGE 21: FACE OFF

A. Billy Jones. B. Lee Cattermole. C. Jack Rodwell. D. Steven Fletcher. E. Vito Mannone. F. Patrick van Aanholt. G. John O'Shea. H. Charis Mavrias. I. Connor Wickham.

PAGE 28: NICKNAME THAT CLUB

A. Swansea City, The Swans. B. Hull City, The Tigers. C. Southampton, The Saints. D. Everton, The Toffees. E. West Ham United, The Hammers. F. Manchester United, The Red Devils. G. Newcastle United, The Magpies. H. Leicester City, The Foxes. I. Arsenal, The Gunners. J. Stoke City, The Potters.

PAGE 47: SAMSON'S SUMS

1. 19. 2. 26. 3. 38. 4. 5. 5. 5. 6. 19. 7. 56. 8. 9. 9. 2. 10. 11

PAGE 60: TEST YOURSELF ON 2014

1. Adam Johnson. 2. Fabio Borini. 3. Lee Cattermole. 4. Portugal. 5. Ki & Marcos Alonso. 6. Birmingham City. 7. Liam Bridcutt & Will Buckley. 8. Costel Pantilimon & Jack Rodwell. 9. Jordi Gomez. 10. Jack Rodwell. 11. Swansea City. 12. Kidderminster Harriers. 13. Adam Johnson. 14. Adam Johnson & Connor Wickham.

CONTENTS

Published by

Pedigree®

Books Ltd

under licence from
BRITISH SKY BROADCASTING

Pedigree Books Ltd
The Old Rectory
Matford Lane
Exeter
Devon EX2 4PS
© 2000

All editorial, design and repro by
Final Score Ltd.
finalscore@compuserve.com
Pictures: Action Images and Allsport
with special thanks to Gavin, Paul,
Shazad and Sarah.

£6.99

WELCOME TO

SKY SPORTS FOO

IN THE PAST YEAR Sky Sports has continued to lead the way in the coverage of sport worldwide with over 25,000 hours of action from a multitude of sports. From football to greyhound racing Sky Sports' coverage is beyond compare.

Wherever the action is, Sky is never far away. In fact, more than any other broadcaster, Sky has been at the centre of all the passion and drama from so many live events, so many different sports, in so many parts of the world.

Whilst there has been so much to admire and applaud in the world of sport over the last year, certain images are still vivid; all brought to life by Sky's wonderful team of presenters, commentators, cameramen and behind-the-scenes experts.

Football, inevitably, is such an important part of the Sky Sports package - and that is indicated by the coverage extended to the beautiful game in this the second Sky Sports Annual.

And what a football season it proved to be. Manchester United were worthy winners of the Premiership, but credit also goes to Arsenal, Leeds, Liverpool and Chelsea for making the race for the first title of the new millennium one to remember for a long time.

The current Premiership season is already living up to expectations and the resurgence of Manchester City as well as the return to top flight action of Charlton and Ipswich has added even more intrigue and entertainment to this great competition.

Beyond the money-spinning world of football, there was much to enjoy in so many other areas of the sporting arena. Lennox Lewis, all power and grace, continued to dominate the heavyweight division in boxing whilst Prince Naseem Hamed added stamina to the style which has made him the number one flyweight in the world. Sky Box office fight fans have had a wonderful year of entertainment.

And what about the English Rugby Union side who secured a memorable Test match victory against the Springboks? We pay tribute to Clive Woodward's magnificent men; just as we acknowledge the achievements of so many teams and individuals who have made the last year of sport a great one.

Sky Sports celebrate 10 years of top level broadcasting in 2001 and you can be certain that wherever and whenever there is a sporting occasion to savour, Sky Sports' cameras will be right at the heart of the action, where it counts.

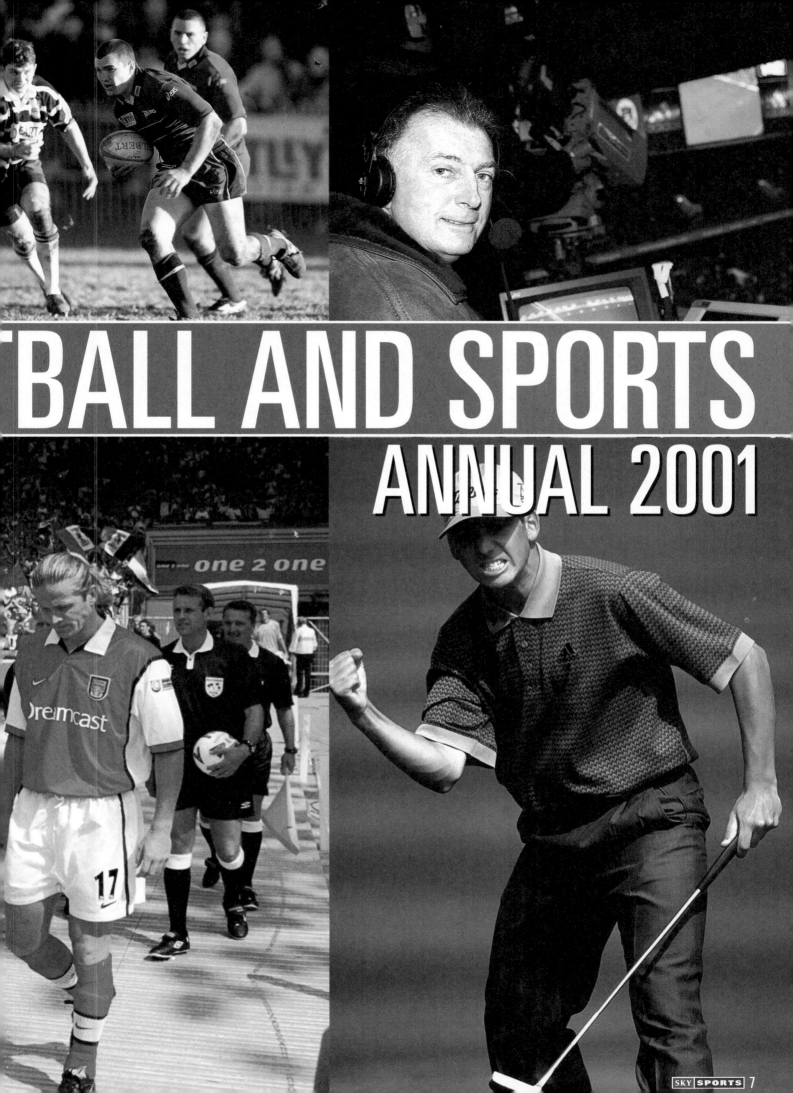

BALL AND SPORTS

ANNUAL 2001

SKY TV FOR THAT

SKY SPORTS

WINNING COVERAGE

SKY TV FOR THAT WINNING COVERAG

CARLING CHAMPIONS

SKY SPORTS

ACTION ZONE

FEATURING: RUGBY LEAGUE, RUGBY UNION, CRICKET & BASKETBALL

LOVE THIS GAME!

Super League slogan sums up the popularity of Rugby

WHILE there was much dismay when Gateshead Thunder folded after just one season in Super League and Sheffield Eagles merged with Huddersfield, rugby league in England has still grown considerably over the last 20 years.

Expansion may have failed in south Wales, Kent, the east Midlands, and the north east, and while London continue to struggle, the major clubs in Super League are still getting bigger and better.

By importing a competitive team from Gateshead, Hull FC gave the city's passionate black-and-white fans something to cheer; Leeds' crowds remained impressive despite struggling at the start of 2000 on the field; Wigan followers got used to life in their new JJB stadium and Bradford remained the club to match both on and off the paddock.

The Super League play-off system has also proved hugely popular: the average post-season crowd in 1999 was 19,654, almost three times as many who watched the old Premiership games 20 years ago.

League is getting bigger at each end of the spectrum - over 50,000 fans have been at Old Trafford for each of the Grand Finals, Northern Ford Premiership crowds were booming in 2000, and more and more amateur clubs are being formed across the whole country.

The Super League slogan says 'Love This Game' - thousands of people around the country already do.

SUPER LEAGUE SPECIAL

Packing 'EM IN

How average crowds have increased

CLUB	1979-80	1990-91	1999
LEEDS RHINOS	6,681	11,102	13,703
BRADFORD BULLS	6,236	5,274	13,398
WIGAN WARRIORS	4,665	14,493	9,466
ST HELENS	5,577	7,391	8,460
HULL FC	10,021	6,699	7,183
CASTLEFORD TIGERS	3,714	6,019	6,877
WARRINGTON WOLVES	5,122	5,915	5,110
HALIFAX BLUESOX	4,090	7,181	4,483
SALFORD CITY REDS	4,846	3,785	4,505
WAKEFIELD TRINITY	4,559	4,848	4,235
HUDDERSFIELD-SHEFFIELD GIANTS	1654'*	4,031+	4,018
LONDON BRONCOS	6,096'	724'	2,935
LEAGUE AVERAGE:	4,875	5,962	6,278

Hudd-Sheff and Hull crowds are from 2000. When clubs were not in top division until a year later, the top flight attendances have been given.
' = in Division Two; * = Huddersfield. + = Sheffield.

* More Rugby League action over the page as we turn the spotlight on Leon Pryce

Super League rugby - full of thrills, skills and spills

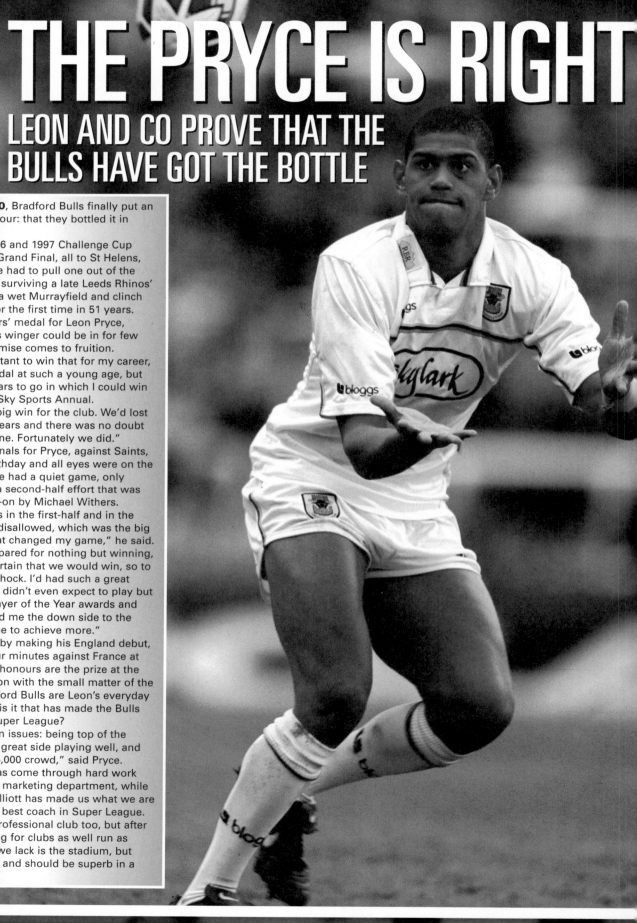

THE PRYCE IS RIGHT

LEON AND CO PROVE THAT THE BULLS HAVE GOT THE BOTTLE

ON APRIL 29, 2000, Bradford Bulls finally put an end to a vicious rumour: that they bottled it in major Finals.

Having lost the 1996 and 1997 Challenge Cup Finals and the 1999 Grand Final, all to St Helens, Matthew Elliott's side had to pull one out of the bag. And they did it, surviving a late Leeds Rhinos' rally to win 24-18 at a wet Murrayfield and clinch the Challenge Cup for the first time in 51 years.

It was a first winners' medal for Leon Pryce, but the exciting Bulls winger could be in for few more if his early promise comes to fruition.

"It was quite important to win that for my career, to get a winners' medal at such a young age, but hopefully I've got years to go in which I could win medals," Pryce told Sky Sports Annual.

"But it was a very big win for the club. We'd lost three Finals in four years and there was no doubt we had to win that one. Fortunately we did."

The first of those Finals for Pryce, against Saints, came on his 18th birthday and all eyes were on the Yorkshire flyer. But he had a quiet game, only bursting to life with a second-half effort that was ruled out for a knock-on by Michael Withers.

"I was very nervous in the first-half and in the second I had the try disallowed, which was the big turning point. But that changed my game," he said.

"All week I had prepared for nothing but winning, I was 100 per cent certain that we would win, so to lose was a massive shock. I'd had such a great season - at the start I didn't even expect to play but I won both Young Player of the Year awards and then boom! It showed me the down side to the game and inspired me to achieve more."

Pryce did end 1999 by making his England debut, scoring after only four minutes against France at Hull. Again, England honours are the prize at the end of the 2000 season with the small matter of the World Cup. But Bradford Bulls are Leon's everyday occupation. So what is it that has made the Bulls the biggest club in Super League?

"There are two main issues: being top of the League and having a great side playing well, and having an average 15,000 crowd," said Pryce.

"But that support has come through hard work over the years by the marketing department, while our coach Matthew Elliott has made us what we are on the pitch. He's the best coach in Super League.

"Leeds are a very professional club too, but after that you are struggling for clubs as well run as ours. The only thing we lack is the stadium, but Odsal is being rebuilt and should be superb in a couple of years."

Pryce in typical barnstorming action

Leon wants to be ENGLAND'S BEST

PRYCE, who first mixed with the Bulls first team when he was taken to their training camp in Lanzarote aged just 15, watches Aussie League on Sky every weekend and still dreams of playing in the white-hot atmosphere Down Under.

He'd also love to work with his childhood hero, Ellery Hanley. But for now, he wants to be the best player in England.

"It is my dream and ambition to play in Australia - that's what I'm working towards," he admits. "But you have to be at your best to play there so it won't be for a couple more years yet. The timing is important - you have to go at the right time for the club signing you and for yourself.

"We haven't got as many Aussies at Bradford as some clubs but playing with someone like Brad Mackay shows me how good you have to be. He's a great player and as long as the Aussies coming over are top players, that's great. But if you have too many mediocre players, no better than the local lads, then it spoils it for the young kids. Imagine if we'd had Wendell Sailor on the wing? I'd never have got a game."

With the ultimate goal in mind - a starring role in the NRL - Pryce is putting in the work in the gym and cutting out the fast food.

"I love burgers but I don't eat them all the time!" said the 15 stone, 6ft 1in giant.

"We have a conditioning coach and he makes sure I eat the right things. And we do weights three or four times a week. That has made us tough and hard. We are the biggest, strongest and fastest team, but that is no use if you can't play rugby!"

* Now turn over for a spotlight on the 15-a-side version of rugby.

Bradford finally ended their Cup Final jinx with a Challenge Cup win over Leeds

RUGBY UNION

ENGLAND'S dramatic 27-22 victory over the Springboks in the summer - so giving them a share of the spoils in the series - was only their third Test win ever in South Africa.

The home nation claimed the only try of the game in the last minute to set the nerves on edge, but England were worthy winners with Jonny Wilkinson the undisputed hero.

England's ace kicker deservedly claimed the man of the match award with eight penalties and a drop goal to seal a memorable win - and the Springboks could have no complaints.

Clive Woodward's battlers finally got revenge for their World Cup exit at the hands of South Africa in gutsy fashion to record a victory which meant they could be taken seriously as a major force in world rugby.

England were rock-solid and were unlucky to concede a last-ditch try by Joost van der Westhuizen, but Wilkinson's magic kicking - along with tremendous fighting spirit - was the difference between the two teams.

The match was by no means a classic, but was characterised by tough battles among the forwards, with awesome defence from both sides. And it was somewhat fitting that England completed their hat-trick of wins on South African soil in Bloemfontein, known as South Africa's City of Roses.

HAIL WOODWARD'S WARRIORS

The MATCH STATS

SOUTH AFRICA 22-27 ENGLAND
2nd Test, Bloemfontein

SOUTH AFRICA:
Tries: Joost van der Westhuizen.
Conversions: Percy Montgomery (1).
Penalties: Braam Van Straaten (4), Percy Montgomery (1).

ENGLAND:
Tries: nil. **Conversions:** nil.
Penalties: Jonny Wilkinson (8).
Drop goals: Wilkinson (1)

RUGBY UNION

ENGLAND'S PREVIOUS TRIUMPHS IN THE SOUTHERN HEMISPHERE

England's win in Bloemfontein was their third away to South Africa and only their fifth ever against the Southern Hemisphere giants of the Springboks, Australia and New Zealand:-

Year	Opponents	Venue	Score
1972	**S.Africa**	Johannesburg	18-9
1973	**N.Zealand**	Auckland	16-10
1994	**S.Africa**	Pretoria	32-15
1995	**Australia**	Capetown	25-22
2000	**S.Africa**	Bloemfontein	27-22

JONNY WILKINSON'S superb 27-point haul in Bloemfontein took him to within 118 points of Rob Andrew's all-time England scoring record of 396. A remarkable achievement so early in his international career.

It is hard to imagine that England have ever discovered a player with such all-round match-winning talent and at that stage he was averaging an impressive 14 points a Test.

Wilkinson was typically modest and cool about arguably his finest achievement while the rugby world raved about the manner in which he left South Africa floundering.

A missed kick, a rarity indeed, would have equalled a world record but that was of little concern to Wilkinson who was playing his first game for two months.

He said afterwards: "I have never known a game where there was such a feeling of tiredness after 20 minutes. I had to dig deep - training at altitude is one thing, but playing in it is another.

"We failed a few times against teams like South Africa in the past, but I feel that we've now paid something back. It was a great result for us."

Coach Clive Woodward praised his hero, saying: "We missed him when we lost the first Test in Pretoria, and it was an awesome performance by Jonny. But, as ever, he took it all in his stride."

WILKINSON
PUTS BOKS TO THE SWORD

FUN TIME!

TEST YOUR SPORTING KNOWLEDGE BY TACKLING THE SKY SPORTS CROSSWORD AND PUZZLES

CROSSWORD

CLUES ACROSS

7 Home of Surrey Cricket Club (4)
8 Speedy rival of Super Bike ace Carl Fogarty (6)
10 Nationality of footballer Sami Hyypia and Formula One's Mika Hakkinen (7)
11 Former New Zealand All Black - Batty (5)
12 Chess piece also known as a Castle (4)
13 American golfer, Craig (5)
17 Birmingham City footballer who looks after his money (5)
18 Oriental form of boxing (4)
22 The Rhinos of Rugby League (5)
23 Many European stadia are called this (7)
24 Famous jug the Britsh Open Champion receives (6)
25 See 5 Down (4)

CLUES DOWN

1 The Reds of Rugby League (7)
2 Replaced Lawrence Dallaglio as England's Rugby Union skipper (7)
3 Venue for the Champions League Final 2000 (5)
4 Dubious sounding baseball team from Los Angeles (7)
5 and 25 Across Welterweight boxing champ ... de la -. (5,4)
6 Sam Torrance, Ian Woosnam and Lee Westwood, for example (5)
9 Famous motor racing track in middle England (9)
14 Irish Rugby Union team which reached the European Cup Final (7)
15 Former footballer Lee or ex-motor racing ace Roger (7)
16 Vinny Jones, formally (7)
19 Neath's Rugby Union side play in this colour (5)
20 A treasured possession of every sportsman (5)
21 Controversial heavyweight boxer (5)

Answers on page 92

THE NAME GAME

Study the sets of clues below and when you've identified the sportsman or woman in question place their initials into the relevant boxes to come up with the name of a top golfer.

2 & 6 Pocket-sized Welsh golfer with a big heart

9 & 8 Young Premiership football manager who made a big impression last season

4 & 7 Didn't make such a good impression and was sacked as manager of Wimbledon

10 & 3 Top Indian batsman who probably relaxes around the old camp fire

1 & 5 Nottinghamshire batsman, one of the longest-serving cricketers in the English game

1	2	3	4	5	6	7	8	9	10

WHO R U?

The sports are obvious, but we need to know the names of these three female stars.

MISSING LINK

Using the two words shown in each case as a clue, fit the name of a famous sportsman (or woman) in the middle to form two popular phrases (see example). Clue: the spellings may not always be correct!

1 CARL	**LEWIS**	CARROLL (Athletics)
2 SHIRT		HOLE (Motor Racing)
3 BROKEN		ATTACK (Football)
4 HARD		WORK (Rugby Union)
5 SAINT		BEARER (Rugby League)
6 SHINING		HAWK (Cricket)

CRYPTIC QUIZ

Solve the following cryptic clues about well-known sporting figures and then, using the initial letter of each surname, fill in the boxes below to come up with a fighting weight in boxing.

1 Alarm bells should ring when this spin king is on form
2 Does he drive the fastest golf buggy in the west?
3 You've got to be thick-skinned to play for this rugby league club
4 A lot of people have named their dogs after this awesome athlete
5 Cross this club chairman and it could prove deadly
6 Ronnie O'Sullivan's quick-fire nickname

1	2	3	4	5	6

Turning it ON

Schofield, the 6ft 2in blond from Rochdale, is not the only great young spinner on the Test circuit. Every country seems to have one nowadays;

DANIEL VETTORI
New Zealand and Northern Districts age 21

The curly-haired Kiwi student caught the eye with some superb displays in England in 1999. His glasses disguised a clever and determined bowler who rarely strays in accuracy.

BRIAN MURPHY
Zimbabwe and Western Province age 23

Played most of his cricket in South Africa but returned to his homeland and made his international debut in 2000. An accurate wrist spinner, he caused the West Indies problems on tour.

SAQLAIN MUSHTAQ
Pakistan and Surrey age 23

Took his 200th one-day international wicket at 22. His nagging length and line, his deadly movement from leg to off and his dazzling flight make him almost unplayable when he's on song.

SCHOFIELD
A STAR IN THE MAKING

EVEN AUSSIE WIZARD SHANE WARNE RECKONS CHRIS IS THE BUSINESS

NOT MANY cricketers get their first England cap at 21-years-old. But then Chris Schofield is not any old cricketer. In fact, he's a very young but hugely talented leg spin bowler and England selectors decided that the Lancashire lad was worth a gamble, something they have rarely done in recent years.

Schofield has been monitored as he came through the England Under-19s team and was handed a contract by the ECB before he'd earned his club cap.

With his Lancashire team-mate Andrew Flintoff also in the England side at 21, Schofield should not be lonely, but then he's confident enough without needing the support of his mate 'Fred' or Michael Atherton, another Lancastrian given an England chance in his early 20s.

Schofield is right-handed, spins with his wrist, pitches from leg to off, can turn it on grass or dust and takes wickets. He can bat too. So what's the catch? There is none according to Shane Warne and he should know!

"He's got all the toys," said the Australian spin king.

Schofield won a lot of praise on the England A tour of Bangladesh and New Zealand in 1999, impressing with his ability and attitude. Some critics think he's cocky but he just believes he can play at the highest level.

"I think he's a very exciting prospect," said England A coach Martyn Moxon. "We've got a young man who's full of enthusiasm, and has a great deal of ability. Hopefully, we can turn that into what's needed at Test level. He's the sort of lad who'll learn by playing. He's confident without being arrogant."

After all the build-up, Schofield had about the quietest debut anyone has ever had for England. He got a duck and did not bowl a ball in the thrashing of Zimbabwe at Lords in May. But he at least got to know what it feels like to play in an England win!

"I used to try to bowl six different balls per over," admits Schofield, who wears sun glasses when bowling to stop him squinting. "I'd bowl a full-length straight one, a leg spinner, a flipper, try a googly and a short one.

"I was just trying to see if I could mix it up and confuse the batsman but then I realised I didn't have to do that. Put five on the spot and one different one - that will get you more wickets."

RED HOT!

LANCASHIRE LADS ARE THE TEAM TO FEAR

A TON OF TALENT

Lancashire had ten England internationals - and Indian batting star Saurav Ganguly - in the 2000 season. Here's a run down on the Red Rose county's home grown stars who have made Lancs the one-day team to fear.

MICHAEL ATHERTON

One of the youngest ever captains of his country, Athers led England a record 52 times in the 1990s. Recovered from a back injury to return with a bang for Lancs and win back his role as England opener.

NEIL FAIRBROTHER

One of the best one-day batsman England has ever seen, 'Harvey' averaged 39.5 in 13 years at the top, even succeeding when all others failed in the 1999 World Cup. But it was not the end to his England career he'd hoped for. After 11 Cup Finals and nine one day titles with Lancashire, he can hardly complain.

JOHN CRAWLEY

Feeding on the responsibility of captaincy, Crawley responded superbly to being dropped by England. His 611 one-day runs helped Lancs win the National League in 1999. 'Creepy' could get a national recall but his dream is to win the County Championship with Lancashire.

ANDREW FLINTOFF

April 2000 was a good month for 'Fred', his beloved Preston North End won the Second Division and he won an England contract. Explosive with the bat and accurate with the ball, at 22-years-old , he has time to become one of England's greatest all-rounders.

IAN AUSTIN

MIKE WATKINSON

PETER MARTIN

NEIL FAIRBROTHER

ANDY FLINTOFF

GLEN CHAPPLE

MIKE ATHERTON

JOHN CRAWLEY

PETER MARTIN

Once an England regular, 'Digger' has failed to improve on the exciting fast bowler who took 4-60 in South Africa five years ago. One of the best tail-enders on the circuit, he is more than useful in Lancs' pace attack.

WARREN HEGG

Little wicketkeeper who was unlucky to be behind Jack Russell when he was keeping at his peak. Finally got England honours on the Ashes tour when he was already 30. A fine one-day batsman too.

IAN AUSTIN

Bully's economic and incredibly accurate bowling for over a decade for Lancs was rewarded with an England call up in 1998. Had a great start to his international career, but disappointed in the World Cup. Superb and consistent for his county; he can also fling the bat to good effect.

GRAHAM LLOYD

A short-lived, disastrous England one-day career ended when he averaged only 8, but he had a fine 1999 for Lancs, averaging 42 in the Championship and 35 in the one-days. Solid rather than exciting middle-order bat.

CHRIS SCHOFIELD

The England Under-19 star filled the gap left by Sri Lankan spin king Muralitharan and underlined his potential with 8-116 against Gloucester in his debut season and 82 wickets in just ten matches as Lancs finished second in the 1999 Championship.

GLEN CHAPPLE

This fast bowler from Yorkshire was tipped for England honours after some thrilling bursts for Lancashire but failed to develop at the same pace and has yet to add to his England A honours. At 26, he still is young in cricketing terms and is a great strike bowler at county level.

MIKE WATKINSON

Veteran all-rounder who became player-coach to the second team in 2000. Was an effective pinch-hitter and spin bowler for England, as well as a medium-pace seamer on the county circuit.

IT'S ALL COMING UP ON

SKY SPORTS

JANUARY 2001

10 Worthington Cup	Semi-final 1st leg
17 Worthington Cup	Semi-final 2nd leg
28 NFL	Super Bowl XXXV

FEBRUARY 2001

22-26 International cricket	Sri Lanka v England 1st Test
25 Worthington Cup Final	

MARCH 2001

3 Lloyds TSB Six Nations	England v Scotland
7-11 International cricket	Sri Lanka v England 2nd Test
10 FA Cup 6th Round	
15-19 International cricket	Sri Lanka v England 3rd Test
17 FA Cup 6th Round replay	
22-25 US PGA Tour Golf	The Players' Championship
23 International cricket	Sri Lanka v England 1st one-day international
25 International cricket	Sri Lanka v England 2nd one-day international
27 International cricket	Sri Lanka v England 3rd one-day international

APRIL 2001

7 Lloyds TSB Six Nations	England v France
8 FA Cup Semi-Final	

MAY 2001

6 FA Carling Premiership	The final day of the season
12 FA Cup Final	
26 Nationwide League Division 3	Play-off Final
27 Nationwide League Division 2	Play-off Final
28 Nationwide League Division 1	Play-off Final

JUNE 2001

14-17 US PGA Tour Golf	US Open

AUGUST 2001

16-19 US PGA Tour Golf	PGA Championship

SEPTEMBER 2001

27-30 International Golf	Ryder Cup

NOVEMBER 2001

1-4 US PGA Tour Golf	THE TOUR Championship

Stay in touch with Sky Sports as the sporting year unfolds

SKY SPORTS BASKETBALL REVIEW

What a sporting year it was for the city of Manchester. In the football arena, United celebrated another Premiership triumph whilst neighbours City secured their return to the top flight with automatic First Division promotion. Meanwhile, on the basketball court Manchester Giants were sweeping all before them and sending records tumbling in the wonderfully-named Dairylea Dunkers Championship.

CHAMPIONS 1999/2000

MANC-NIFICENT

Giants shooting guard Phil Handy calling the plays

Tony Holley pro with a laying-u he leaves opponents groun

IT WAS the year that Manchester finally cast off more than a decade of under-achievement, reaching all three finals and winning a record 45 games - and then had their American owners pull out within hours of their Championship triumph at Wembley!

The Giants have always been a British basketball soap opera but brilliant young American coach Nick Nurse seemed to have finally rid them of the under-achievers tag as Manchester lost narrowly in the Finals of the National Cup and uni-ball Trophy before rebounding to win the Northern Conference and the Play-Off Final against his former club Birmingham.

Owners, the Cook Group, chose that moment to announce they were to withdraw their backing, alleging an increase in rent at their MEN Arena home was behind their decision.

Happily, within days, a number of potential new backers had been identified who were keen to keep top flight basketball in one of Britain's leading sporting cities. And while that made for a long summer of uncertainty, at least the Giants fans could hold onto the memories of some of the best basketball seen in this country in years.

"That just about summed up two crazy years being in charge of this team," said Nurse. "And the unfortunate thing is, in all the fuss, people seem to have forgotten that we won a Championship on the final day.

"It was nice to be able to rid ourselves of that tag of 'nearly men'. Yes, we lost two Cup Finals but I just think that at Wembley some of the luck we've been lacking finally turned our way."

Slam Dunk! An easy score for Giants' guard Travis Conlan

Manchester's Roy Hairston gets the better of the Towers defence

MANCHESTER RULE THE ROOST IN BASKETBALL AS WELL AS FOOTBALL

The Player of the Year, Tony Dorsey, with his Most Valuable Player award from the Dairylea Dunkers Championship Final

Story of the SEASON

THE TONE for the season was set on the opening day, when the Giants welcomed arch rivals the Sheffield Sharks to the MEN Arena and beat them 86-79, the start of a run of just two defeats in 22 games.

One of those losses came at the London Leopards who responded to a rare win during a difficult start to the campaign by sacking Billy Mims, the only coach they had ever had, replacing him with larger than life Bob Donewald who presided over the rest of a disappointing season for the team.

Defeat number three for the Giants was a costly one, however, as the Sheffield Sharks stormed back from a strong Manchester start to hold on to their National Cup crown, 89-80 at Sheffield.

Nurse's team, led by the ever-impressive Tony Dorsey, steady point guard Travis Conlan and athletic American forward Roy Hairston, then embarked on another 15-game winning run, ended at the MEN Arena by the London Towers whose shock 89-76 win indicated that they were hitting form at the right time.

They proved it a fortnight later, at the NIA Arena, Birmingham, when they won a heart-stopping uni-ball Trophy Final encounter with the Giants 74-73 thanks to 17 points from MVP Danny Lewis. The outcome was only decided on the buzzer, however, when Manchester failed to get off a shot inside the final 25 seconds.

While the Towers were running away with the Southern Conference title - they would win it by five games from second placed Thames Valley - Manchester and Sheffield were heading for another dramatic title chase in the North.

That battle provided countless twists and turns in the closing weeks, although the Giants' emphatic 84-59 win at Sheffield in late March appeared to have tied up the title for Nurse's crew.

Three days later, it was advantage Sharks as Manchester slumped surprisingly at Thames Valley. But April Fool's Day proved no laughing matter for Sharks coach Chris Finch as his side were downed at lowly Newcastle, handing Nurse the title. To rub salt into Sheffield's wounds, the Giants went down 99-78 at Chester 24 hours later. Plain crazy!

By the time the teams met at the MEN on the final day of the regular season, the outcome was academic although Manchester underlined their superiority by taking an over-time thriller 104-93.

In a thrilling Wembley finale Nurse took on his former college friend Finger, the man he had recommended for the Birmingham job when he himself left the Bullets three years ago.

The Final proved a tense and bruising affair with former Giant Emiko Etete keeping the Bullets in contention with a solid 13-point performance but, inevitably, Tony Dorsey helped out Manchester when they needed him most, his 22 points clinching a 74-65 win.

SKY SPORTS BASKETBALL REVIEW

Where the HONOURS WENT

GAME OF THE SEASON:
London Towers 74 Manchester Giants 73, uni-ball Trophy Final

The best in the south beat the best in the north in a thriller at the NIA Arena in Birmingham. The final see-sawed dramatically and the Giants, with 25 seconds left on the clock, had one final chance to win the game. But London's impressive defence stood firm and did not even let the Giants get off a shot.

TEAM OF THE SEASON
The Manchester Giants

Comparisons with Manchester United have always stopped short in one area - the moneybags Giants have never been winners ... until now. All that changed in spectacular fashion as the Giants reached three Finals, clinched the all-important Championship and won a record 45 games in all competitions.

PLAYER OF THE SEASON
Tony Dorsey, Manchester Giants

He ended the season averaging 23.2 points and 7.6 rebounds a game, but that only told part of the story about the 29-year-old American. Dorsey enhanced his reputation as a big game player and there was no stopping him at Wembley where he won his third Championship MVP title.

COACH OF THE SEASON
Nick Nurse, Manchester Giants

The most high-pressure job in British basketball and Nurse, in his second year in charge, delivered the goods where so many had failed before him. The best record in the League and the Northern Conference title were followed by a comfortable victory at Wembley.

BAD BOY OF THE SEASON
Bob Donewald, London Leopards

On top of the usual technical fouls, ejections and suspensions came a charge of insulting referees after a game for one of the game's wildest coaches. Bob was also warned to tone down his entrances after roaring in to a game on a motorbike.

Dairylea Dunkers Northern Conference: Manchester Giants
Dairylea Dunkers Southern Conference: London Towers
Dairylea Dunkers Championship: Manchester Giants
National Cup: Sheffield Sharks
uni-ball Trophy: London Towers
League MVP Award: Tony Dorsey (Manchester Giants)

No pressure! Towers Danny Lewis at the free throw line as he hits the game winning shot in the uni-ball Trophy Final

Big bad Bob Donewald talks things over with his rebounding ace Brandon Brantley

It's that simple, Nick Nurse draws out the plays for his team

The sweet taste of success for the Towers as they edged out the Giants in the closest uni-ball Trophy Final in history.

FOOTBALL ZONE

FEATURING: TRIBUTES TO MAN UNITED, CHELSEA, LEICESTER & RANGERS... ANDY GRAY'S A-Z OF STARS... REVIEW OF THE 1999-2000 SEASON... THE FUNNY SIDE OF SOCCER... WEMBLEY MARES

MANCHESTER UNITED: FA CARLING

It's a FACT

United scored four goals on no fewer than 10 occasions last season and hit four against Bradford and West Ham TWICE.

United have now won the Premiership title six times in the eight years since its inception in 1992. And in the two seasons they didn't win it, they finished second.

United set a new record for the number of goals scored in a Premiership campaign (82 by Newcastle in 1994) with four games remaining. They finished the season with 97.

United scored more goals at home than title rivals Liverpool, Leeds and Chelsea recorded home AND away last season.

THE GREATEST
SIR ALEX HAILS HIS Y2K CHAMPIONS A

BETTER than the Busby Babes, greater than the 1968 kings of Europe; Sir Alex Ferguson sparked a whole new debate when he declared his all-conquering class of 2000 as the best Manchester United side the club have ever produced.

That's some accolade, by anybody's standards and whether you agree with Sir Alex or not, there's certainly no arguing with the fact that his current Champions are the best in the country by a mile, and likely to stay at the top for a while to come.

The United manager was clearly on a title winning high when he produced his emphatic statement about the stature of his team, despite the loss of their European Cup crown.

"This is the best United team ever," said Ferguson. "It is a tremendous achievement after winning the treble last season. I've no doubt players like Law, Best and Charlton would still have been great in this era, but the way this team has continued to grow makes them, for me, the best this club has seen.

"There were some who, at the start of the season, suggested that having scaled the heights last year we would lack the hunger for it again. Some even said it was time I resigned because we couldn't go on from there. That was ridiculous.

"The players have proved their determination and desire to keep on winning by taking this title. The camaraderie is just growing stronger as most of the

EMIERSHIP CHAMPIONS 1999-2000

OF ALL TIME

UNITED'S BEST EVER

players are still coming to their footballing peak."

Even before LAST season had concluded, the bookmakers had already installed United as 4-6 favourites to win the title THIS season. Fergie supported the bookies by declaring: "There is even better to come from this team." A frightening prospect indeed for the rest.

Ferguson's own hunger for success shows no signs of diminishing either and, after equalling Bob Paisley's record of six League titles, his sights are firmly set on more trophies.

"At 58, a manager could easily go about things in a more sedate manner and be less aggressive. In many ways I am a more mellow person but, if the players have the drive, I can enjoy that drive," he concluded.

MANCHESTER UNITED: FA CARLING

YORKE HAILS UNITED FAITHFUL

SOME weeks before United had wrapped up their sixth Premiership title, Sir Alex Ferguson had been critical of an Old Trafford crowd he claimed didn't get behind the team enough.

But whilst the United boss claimed certain home supporters 'were more interested in eating crisps' than encouraging the players, striker Dwight Yorke thanked the fans for their vocal backing.

The Trinidad and Tobago star, who claimed his second successive Premiership medal, said: "It has been another brilliant season for us and we are all delighted to have put on some quality shows for our fans.

"They have always played a great part in our success. In the two years I've been here they have been fantastic and they have also showed their quality. It is just great to be a part of it.

"It was always going to be difficult coming off a season like last year but if someone said we were going to win the League again - we certainly would have taken it.

"This is one of the trophies we always set out to win - we know where our priorities lie. To win the League again is tremendous and all credit to the players."

And the fans, of course!

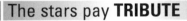

The stars pay TRIBUTE

"Sir Alex is the toughest, hungriest, meanest and most cussed competitor I've ever met in the whole of my football life. To be any use to him, you have to be a winner. Every sacrifice is worth it for the benefit of the club. For him there is no other agenda" **STEVE BRUCE**

"United are still young enough to go on dominating and the rest of us have to face up to the task of trying to overtake them. This will not be Sir Alex's last triumph and there is every likelihood of him going out in a blaze of glory and winning the Premiership in both of his remaining years at the club" **BRYAN ROBSON**

"I've got total admiration for United and Sir Alex Ferguson. They are way above everyone else in England. The problem now is what do the other clubs do to catch up with them? They have the financial power and player strength to get bigger and bigger" **MARTIN O'NEILL**

"They are in a different league; the best team because they have been so consistent. They deserve credit and it will be interesting to see how we can compete with them. We want to bridge the gap with United. At the moment they are out of everybody's reach" **GIANLUCA VIALLI.**

"They are well ahead of anyone else in the Premiership and I still think they are the best team in Europe, despite their defeat by Real Madrid. They have five or six youngsters who are not going to hit their peak until they're 28 or 29 and they will go from strength to strength" **GLENN HODDLE**

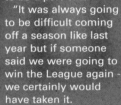

PREMIERSHIP CHAMPIONS 1999-2000

GIGGS
BACK TO HIS BEST

AFTER bursting on to the scene in such dramatic fashion as a teenager, the fast maturing Ryan Giggs has had to be content with playing a supporting role to the likes of Beckham, Yorke, Scholes and Keane in recent seasons.

But having come to terms with the 'new George Best' tag and more recently overcome a hamstring injury which has kept his career in check to some degree, the Welsh winger is flying again.

Since the turn of the year, Giggs has been a revelation and in the last few months of the season was as inspirational, if not more so, than skipper Keane and the brilliant Becks.

Recurring hamstring problems are always a nightmare for players like Giggs whose game is built around sudden bursts of acceleration and sublime changes of direction. They certainly took their toll for a time.

But after finishing last season with a flourish the happy 26-year-old said: "Since we got back from Brazil in January I've been really happy with my form. They say that players peak at 27 or 28 so I expect to be playing the best football of my life in the next couple of years."

One of the main reasons Giggs was able to enjoy a rare, injury-free run was the damage-limiting stretching and exercising routine he now goes through religiously before and after playing.

"It's just a little bit every day before training and after training, just doing various stretches and weights to build up the hamstrings," he explained. "It seems to have done the trick."

CHELSEA
FA CUP WINNERS 2000

THE F.A.

AXA

SPONSORED BY AXA
NNERS 2000
AXA
THE F.A. CUP

IT WON'T go down in history as the greatest FA Cup Final ever, but try telling Chelsea fans the 2000 showdown was a dire encounter.

Gianluca Vialli's men, having blown their other route into Europe via the League, secured a place in the UEFA Cup as Wembley staged its last Final.

For match winner Roberto Di Matteo it was another personal triumph, coming three years after he had scored one of the fastest goals seen beneath the Twin Towers.

His close range strike which settled a tepid affair can hardly be compared to the thunderous strike which set up

victory over Middlesbrough in the 1997 Final, but it was just as important. More so, perhaps.

Chelsea were worthy winners, not even Aston Villa fans could deny that on a day when their team just did not perform, as the boys from the Bridge kept the blue flag flying high.

CHILD'S PLAY FOR

BLUES FINISH ON A HIGH

GIANLUCA VIALLI would have been gutted, and jobless perhaps, had Chelsea failed to deliver at the end of a season which had promised so much.

The Blues boss admitted: "It was a long season of ups and downs - but that was the best way to finish it. I was very pleased for everybody because the players put so much effort into the season. The FA Cup was their reward.

"We didn't have a great season in the Premiership, but I certainly didn't feel any big regrets at being knocked out of

the Champions League in a Quarter-Final by Barcelona. We didn't expect to get that far."

After a disappointing Final which, unusually for Chelsea, few clear cut chances were created, Vialli paid tribute to his defence; Marcel Desailly in particular.

"He did a magnificent job as did all the others in the back four. Marcel was fantastic. He won everything in the air, and we knew that was vital against Dion Dublin. I certainly thought we deserved to win the game - and I'm delighted," said Vialli.

CHELSEA

DAVID BECKHAM and Co had set the trend a couple of weeks earlier by parading their children on the Old Trafford turf as Manchester United celebrated another Premiership triumph.

Well, anything the United boys could do their Chelsea counterparts were determined to do better. Skipper Dennis Wise in particular.

In an unprecedented move, and one not appreciated by Wembley security officers, England midfielder Wise grabbed son Henry on his way up the 39 steps to collect the FA Cup

Balancing the youngster in one arm and holding the trophy somewhat precariously in the other, Wise broke with tradition and secured a famous photograph which will take pride of place in the family album.

Wembley officials took a dim view of the Chelsea captain's unusual celebration which was copied by team-mates Frank Leboeuf and Gus Poyet, who also took their children on the steep climb up to the Royal Box.

Afterwards Wise said: "We all just decided that it would be nice to take the kids up to get the Cup. I'm getting on a bit now at 33 and I might never get the chance to do something like that again.

"I just wanted the boy to come up with me and share it so that when he gets older he can see it all on video."

Wise completed a hat-trick of FA Cup triumphs, having helped Wimbledon to glory in 1988 and skippered Chelsea in 1997. And from start to finish it was child's play against an Aston Villa side which turned up but little else.

Chelsea manager Gianluca Vialli said: "It was good that my players wanted to get their families involved in the success we have. Families are more important even than winning the FA Cup."

View from **THE VILLA CAMP**

ASTON VILLA goalkeeper David James was brave enough to accept the blame for the blunder which led to Roberto di Matteo's winning goal, a close range shot after the Villa No.1 had failed to grasp a Gianfranco Zola free-kick.

"I took my eye off it. It was a silly mistake, what more can I say about it," muttered the distraught former Liverpool number one whose 'Calamity James' tag came back to haunt him.

Villa boss John Gregory, meanwhile, praised his side's effort and refused to heap any more blame on James, whose previous run of good form had led to him being included in Kevin Keegan's preliminary Euro 2000 squad.

"He got us to the Final," said Gregory. "He had done unbelievable things to get us in that position in the first place.

"In the Semi-Final he was outstanding and certainly no criticism can be placed on anybody."

Paul Merson agreed and added: "People make mistakes and he did not mean to do it. If it wasn't for David we would not have reached the Final anyway."

Controversial chairman Doug Ellis warned that Villa will bounce back and said: "This club can achieve so much more.

"I want to win the League. I want to win it next year (2001). This is one of the best Villa squads I have known. We've got a good set of players and I want us to be up there alongside Manchester United."

NOW WHO'S CALLING LEICESTER BORING?

MARTIN O'NEILL'S men shook off their 'boring, boring Leicester' tag to claim the first domestic trophy of the new millennium and so book their passage into Europe in a hugely-entertaining Worthington Cup Final.

Criticised for their negative tactics in the weeks leading up to the February Final, the wily Foxes secured their second trophy in four years as they overcame the brave resistance of Tranmere - after the First Division side had equalised when reduced to ten men.

Leicester's hero was central defender Matt Elliott, a big man for the big occasion, who gave his side the lead after 28 minutes with a towering header from a corner before repeating the feat 12 minutes from the end to clinch victory. All in front of his heavily-pregnant wife.

Elliott had to keep one eye trained on his wife during the Final because he was worried that she would go into labour at any moment.

He admitted in the build-up to the match that he would have pulled out of the game if wife Cathy had started to give birth to their fourth child. The call of nature was put on hold, however, and Cathy was at Wembley to see her husband take centre stage with his match-winning strikes.

It must have been difficult for Scottish international Elliott to concentrate on the game, but he showed true professionalism even though he later admitted: "I had a little panic because I couldn't see her for the first ten minutes, but I managed to keep my eye on her whenever there was a lull in the game. She was jigging around with the best of them at the end.

"Thankfully, scoring the two goals didn't start her off, and everything was okay. It was a wonderful day and another one was just around the corner."

In between Elliott's two goals, David Kelly had given Tranmere hope of an amazing comeback as he struck 15 minutes after replacement referee Phil Richards had sent off Clint Hill for a professional foul on Emile Heskey.

But while Elliott was rightly hailed as the hero, one of many in a Leicester shirt, probably the biggest smile of the day was being worn by Tony Cottee, for whom the victory was even sweeter. Find out why on the next page.

The CUP FINAL LINE-UPS

LEICESTER CITY	TRANMERE ROVERS
Tim **FLOWERS**	Joe **MURPHY**
Frank **SINCLAIR**	Reuben **HAZELL**
Gerry **TAGGART**	Gareth **ROBERTS**
Matt **ELLIOTT**	Clint **HILL**
Steve **GUPPY**	Dave **CHALLINOR**
Stefan **OAKES**	Andy **PARKINSON**
Neil **LENNON**	Gary **JONES**
Muzzy **IZZET**	Nick **HENRY**
Robbie **SAVAGE**	Alan **MAHON**
Tony **COTTEE**	Scott **TAYLOR**
Emile **HESKEY**	David **KELLY**

Referee: **ALAN WILKIE**

Who said **THAT?**

Leicester 'keeper Tim Flowers savoured his personal contribution and said after his first Wembley Final: "I have worked very hard throughout my career to get to this stage. It was a tight game as I thought it would be, but we shaded it."

Northern Ireland midfielder Neil Lennon paid tribute, meanwhile, to what he thought was an outstanding team effort from Leicester. "It is a super day for the boys and the club and the manager," he said. "I thought we were worthy winners on the day. We made some great chances in the second half and could have had three or four."

City boss Martin O'Neill was almost lost for words after seeing his side make up for the agonising defeat by Spurs a year before. He said: "It is every manager's dream to be a winner at Wembley. A magic moment."

Tranmere boss John Aldridge was glowing with pride at the spirit his team had shown to the bitter end. He said: "They have given me enormous satisfaction, not just today but throughout the competition. We showed an awful lot of bottle to get back in the game and I'm proud of them all."

WORTHY WINNERS

WORTHINGTON

TONY COTTEE Leicester

PERSONAL FILE

Date of birth:	11.7.1965
Birthplace:	West Ham
Marital status:	Married to Lorraine
Children:	Chloe (7) and twin boys Matthew and Billy (2)
Car(s):	Range Rover

CAREER FILE

Previous clubs:	West Ham, Everton and Selangor
Domestic honours to date:	One Worthington Cup winners' medal
International honours:	7 England caps. International debut: v Sweden, Sep 1986
Career highlights:	My debuts for West Ham (one goal v Spurs) and Everton (hat-trick v Newcastle)
Biggest disappointment:	Losing the League Cup Final against Spurs in 1999.
Biggest regret:	Being sent off three times, for England Under-21s, West Ham and Everton.
Future ambitions:	To become a player-manager and then a full-time boss.

HERO FILE

Team you supported as a boy:	West Ham
Who was your boyhood idol:	Pele
Current player (in your country) you most admire:	Paul Gascoigne
Current player (outside your country) you most admire:	Ronaldo
Best coach you have played for:	John Lyall at West Ham, both as a coach and a manager
Best game you've played in:	Everton 4 Liverpool 4 in the FA Cup a few years ago. Came on as sub and scored twice.

FAVOURITE FILE

Other sports:	Tennis and snooker
Other sportsman:	Colin Montgomerie
Kind of music:	Soul and dance
Artist or band:	George Michael/Bee Gees
Actor:	Tom Cruise
Movies:	All the 'Carry On' films
Food/wine:	Lasagne/Chardonnay
Fashion designer:	Hugo Boss
Country/city visited:	Bermuda
Holiday destination:	Australia or New Zealand

COTTEE'S A

WINNER at last!

AFTER 17 YEARS OF TRYING 'TC' IS FINALLY TOP DOG

BY ANY STRETCH of the imagination Tony Cottee has had a great career.

He's been scoring goals at the top level (more than 200 in fact) ever since he opened his account on his League debut for West Ham in 1983. An England international with seven caps, he also had the distinction of being the country's most expensive player when he joined Everton for £2 million in the summer of 1988.

But in terms of medals, and not memories, the rewards have not justified the efforts he has displayed throughout his career. So it was little wonder that TC was wearing the biggest smile of all at Wembley

in February as Leicester lifted the Worthington Cup for the second time in three seasons. Top Cat finally got the cream.

"It's certainly been a long time coming," he said, reflecting on the narrow 2-1 win over First Division battlers Tranmere.

"I've done most things in my career and I'm very proud of the fact I've scored over 200 League goals, but not having a winners' medal of any kind to show for my efforts was beginning to get to me.

"When we lost to Spurs in the 1999 League Cup Final I was convinced my last chance to win that elusive medal had gone.

Thankfully, another chance came along and this time I came away from Wembley a winner. It would have been awful to have ended my career empty handed but now I can retire a happy man."

Not just yet though. He fancies another season at the top with Leicester, having been rewarded with a contract extension, before turning his attentions to a player-manager's position somewhere.

"It has always been my ambition to become a manager, but I'd like the opportunity to be a player-boss first even though I'm well aware it is a challenging role,"says Cottee - a winner at last.

FUN TIME!

TEST YOUR FOOTBALL KNOWLEDGE BY TACKLING THE SKY SPORTS CROSSWORD AND PUZZLES

CROSSWORD

CLUES ACROSS

7 It comes after Layer and London (4)
8 American 'keeper who made a name for himself at Leicester (6)
10 Brazilian international who shares his name with a former Middlesbrough import (7)
11 An American footballer in Glasgow, surely not (5)
12 Samassi .... – formerly with West Ham and Ipswich (4)
13 The smiling version of Nicolas Anelka at 1 down (5)
17 One-time European Cup hero for Aston Villa (5)
18 Johnson of Derby (4)
22 Park owned by Jack Walker (5)
23 Father and son at Upton Park (7)
24 'We are red, we are white, we are ...... dynamite' (6)
25 Adebola, big striker at St Andrews (4)

CLUES DOWN

1 Briefly broke Manchester United's stranglehold on the Premiership title (7)
2 .... of contract (7)
3 Sky Sports expert who had to sport a shaved head for a while (5)
4 Frightening lot from Tannadice (7)
5 Former Coventry midfielder, McGrath (5)
6 A test for a young player, perhaps (5)
9 Barnet's run-down home (9)
14 Bradford striker who can blow hot and cold (7)
15 Highly-rated Villa defender (7)
16 The Saints are at home here...for now (7)
19 Road, Huddersfield used to call home (5)
20 Welsh international midfielder, relegated with Sheffield Wednesday last season (5)
21 Controversially sold by West Ham to Leicester (5)

Answers on page 102

CRYPTIC QUIZ

Solve the following cryptic clues about well-known footballing figures and teams and then, using the initial letter of each surname, fill in the boxes to come up with a Third Division club.

1 Tasty player at Anfield who'd go down well with Coventry's Chippo
2 You might toast a successful manager in Scotland with this drink
3 This manager had enough reasons to cheer up last season
4 First Division club which hasn't been too chirpy in recent seasons
5 ET befriended him in the movie; now he's a Scottish international
6 First Division manager just wasn't suited to the Premiership last season

1	2	3	4	5	6

WHO R U?

Can you identify these three top Premiership players? Go to the bottom of the League if you can't!

MISSING LINK

Using the two words shown in each case as a clue, fit the name of a famous sportsman (or woman) in the middle to form two popular phrases (see example). Clue: the spellings may not always be correct!

1 SEE	SURE	THING
2 SNOW		POINT
3 RAW		PARK
4 SMALL		TELLER
5 RAZOR		SHOOTER
6 SILK		STRINGS

THE NAME GAME

Study the sets of clues below and when you've identified the players or managers in question place their initials into the relevant boxes to come up with the name of a striker.

6 & 8 Manager who led Northampton to promotion from Division Three last season
5 Bootham Crescent is their home (first name only)
4 & 7 Former Premiership boss who helped out at Fulham last season
1 & 10 Swedish international who suffered a broken leg last year
9 & 3 French midfielder who was plying his trade at the Stadium of Light last season
11 & 2 Former West Brom player now at Grimsby

1	2	3	4	5	6	7	8	9	10	11

A to Z OF FOO

A is for

Chris ARMSTRONG
who suffered one of the ultimate insults when his own fans turned against him throughout most of last season. Not surprisingly, the Tottenham striker's confidence deserted him during this tortuous spell but Chris had the last laugh by going on a goal spree towards the end of the campaign and making the critics choke on their own cruel words as he recaptured the form that made him one of the top strikers around.

Lorenzo AMORUSO
who led Glasgow Rangers to another Scottish Premiership title and was also an inspiration during the club's brave bid to set the Champions League alight. His defensive partnership with Aussie Craig Moore was one of the keys to Rangers' latest success.

B is for

Michael BRIDGES
who became Leeds' record signing during the summer of 1999 when he joined the Yorkshire club for £5 million from Sunderland after failing to get regular first team recognition at the Stadium of Light. Many people reckoned rookie boss David O'Leary had taken one hell of a gamble on the young striker but it paid off with dividends and Michael finished his first season at Elland Road as the club's leading scorer.

D is for

Paolo DI CANIO
who never ceases to amaze. Whether he's knocking over referees; throwing a typically Italian tantrum or scoring goals mere mortals can only dream of, one thing is guaranteed; there's never a dull moment when Di Canio is around. Just ask his adoring Upton Park public who warmed to the genius of Paul Alcock's favourite player - especially when he produced one of the goals of the season against Wimbledon.

C is for

Alan CURBISHLEY
who succeeded in guiding Charlton Athletic back to the Premiership after a first, dismal season in the top flight, winning the Division One title at a canter and without needing to win any of their last seven games. Such is Curbishley's growing reputation in the world of football management that, by the end of the season, he was being touted as a natural-born successor to Kevin Keegan as coach of England's national side.

Tony COTTEE
who collected his first ever winners medal (Worthington Cup) as a pro after 17 years of trying. And all this after he had been written off in many quarters following his ill-fated move to Malaysia.

ANDY GRAY SAYS
I was one of the lucky ones on a wonderful Sunday afternoon towards the end of last season. Why? Because I was actually present at Upton Park, commentating for Sky Sports, to witness one of THE goals of this - or any other season. Paolo Di Canio's mid-air volley early on in West Ham's Premiership clash with Wimbledon was a world class goal, an astonishing strike and the kind of finish that has people reaching for superlatives. I marvel at his technique and ability time and time again and he is a player that can light up any match.

TBALL SPOTLIGHT ON THE MAIN MEN OF THE YEAR 2000

E is for

Matthew ETHERINGTON
who came through the youth system at Peterborough United and attracted many scouts to London Road before deciding, along with another former Posh youngster Simon Davies, that his future best lay at Tottenham where he has already made impressive strides. He has already shown he has a great career ahead of him.

Matt ELLIOTT
who was the two-goal hero of Leicester's Worthington Cup Final victory over Tranmere and one of the club's leading scorers last season. Not bad for a centre-half usually renowned for preventing goals not scoring them. The giant Scottish international has been Leicester's not-so-secret weapon in attack where Elliott has filled in admirably in the absence of injured strikers.

F is for

Tore Andre FLO
who has so often been the victim of Gianluca Vialli's notorious 'rotation system' at Chelsea but is now recognised as the London club's leading striker. So skilful for such a tall man, the Norwegian striker is an ice-cool finisher and a popular player at Stamford Bridge. He cost the club peanuts but is now classed in the £20million bracket.

G is for

Shaun GOATER
who has become a Maine Road idol after blasting the goals which helped Manchester City secure their second successive promotion and a return to the top flight after an extended absence. The Bermudan striker might look awkward at times but he knows where the goal is. Now he knows where the Premiership is and could be a surprise hit there.

Marco GABBIADINI
who began his career with York City before finding goalscoring fame with Sunderland. A million pound move to Crystal Palace was doomed to failure but 'Marco Goalo' as he was labelled earlier in his career, restored his reputation with Derby, and last season his 20-odd goals were instrumental in Darlington's push for promotion from Division Three.

H is for

Sami HYYPIA
who has been a revelation at the heart of Liverpool's defence since joining the club from Willem II of Holland before the start of the 1999-2000 season. Blessed with the strength of Neil Ruddock, the skill and vision of Alan Hansen and the aerial ability of Ron Yeats, the Finnish international is just the defensive rock Liverpool have been searching for.

ANDY GRAY SAYS
Sami Hyypia was one of the six nominees in the race for the PFA Players' Player of the Year award and you could have made a strong case for him actually winning the prestigious prize which, in the end, went to Roy Keane. He came into a re-shaped Liverpool side and has been cool, calm and collected from the off. A lot of their success has been down to him and the stability he's brought to the side, which is why Gerard Houllier had no hesitation in making him captain in the absence of Jamie Redknapp. He is a real force at the back for The Reds.

I is for

Muzzy IZZET
who was a model of consistency in the Leicester midfield last season and appeared to be on the verge of a break-through into the England squad. But, when Muzzy was continually overlooked, he decided to take up the option of playing for Turkey in the countdown to Euro 2000 - but not before he had been cruelly abused by anti-Turk football fans following the death of two Leeds fans. He rose above that in his normal style.

Paul INCE
who was back to something like his best form after an indifferent spell with Middlesbrough and forced his way back into the England reckoning at a time when many had written him off as an international player. Unfortunately, Boro team-mate Paul Gascoigne was unable to follow the Guvnor's lead.

K is for

Roy KEANE
who was honoured by both his fellow professionals and the country's football writers who named him the undisputed Player of the Year at the end of a season many thought would be his last as a Manchester United player. The whole world and his dog were predicting a move to Italy or Spain but Keane signed a bank-busting £52,000 a week contract before helping the club to yet another title.

Harry KEWELL
who typified the youthful zest, commitment and craft of David O'Leary's young Leeds side which claimed a well-deserved Champions League qualifying spot. Aussie Kewell also helped himself to the PFA Young Player of the Year title whilst finishing third in the Players' Player category. One of the real stars of the season and now valued in the £15 million region.

J is for

Paul JEWELL
who performed the football equivalent of a minor miracle by keeping Bradford in the Premiership against all the odds to finally end the top flight reign of Wimbledon. Jewell, the youngest manager in the Premier, succeeded in communicating his own never-say-die spirit to his players and they were all hailed as heroes after a win against Liverpool on the last day kept them up. Now boss at Wednesday.

L is for

Robert LEE
who was treated like a modern-day leper by former Newcastle boss Ruud Gullit when he stripped him of the captaincy and unceremoniously dumped him in the stiffs until the Dutchman was himself given the cold shoulder by the club. No sooner had Bobby Robson been installed as the new manager than Lee was back in the team and back to his best.

ANDY GRAY SAYS
Although I would have voted for Kevin Phillips, as a fellow striker, it is hard to disagree with the choice of both the PFA and the media in making Roy Keane, Player of the Year. He was outstanding from start to finish in driving everything United have done. Similarly, Harry Kewell had a marvellous season for Leeds and scored some fantastic goals along the way. He was without doubt the Young Player of the Year although there was some strong competition, most notably from his Leeds team-mates, Michael Bridges, Alan Smith and Ian Harte.

ZONE

M is for

Paul MERSON

who continued to win the on-going battle with his various addictions to become such an influential figure in the Aston Villa side which reached the FA Cup Final, only to lose by the odd goal to Chelsea. Merson's form shot him back into the England reckoning even though he said he was quitting international football and there would not have been many arguments if Merse had picked up the Footballer of the Year award.

David MOYES

who led Preston North End to promotion from the Second Division after a nail-biting race for the Championship. Moyes has done a terrific job at Deepdale since taking over from Gary Peters and is one of the most highly-rated young bosses in the game. One of his great achievements has been to get the best out of former Manchester United youth star Jon Macken whose goals were a key to Preston's success. Surely, Moyes is destined for a top job in English football before very long.

O is for

Egil OLSEN

who never really came to terms with the task of keeping the infamous 'Crazy Gang' spirit alive at Wimbledon and ultimately perished - green wellies and all - before the club's final death knell had been sounded. The Norwegian lost the respect of the players, who failed to adapt to his zonal tactics, as the season wore on and he was replaced by Terry Burton with a few matches remaining.

David O'LEARY

who brilliantly masterminded what turned out to be a very demanding campaign for his young Leeds side which finished the season on a high by qualifying for the Champions League, with a creditable third place. The problems surrounding the ill-fated UEFA Cup trip to Galatasaray sadly cast a shadow over what should have been a season of celebration.

N is for

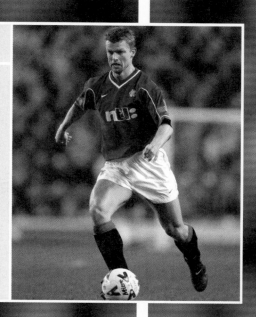

Arthur NUMAN

who more than played his part in Glasgow Rangers' umpteenth League title triumph north of the border. A versatile player with an educated left foot, the Dutch defender has been a good addition to Dick Advocaat's squad since joining the Ibrox club from PSV for £4.5million in the summer of 1998.

P is for

Kevin PHILLIPS

who topped the Premier League scoring charts by plundering an incredible 30 goals in his first season in the top flight. His partnership with Niall Quinn was the key to a very satisfying season for Sunderland and the quality of Phillips' goals, as much as the sheer quantity, earned him second spot in the Player of the Year poll amongst his fellow professionals and a place in Kevin Keegan's England squad for the Euro 2000 competition.

ANDY GRAY SAYS

For my money, Kevin Phillips should have been named Player of the Year because he had an absolutely sensational season in the Premiership - his first at that level, don't forget. To score 30 goals in a side not amongst the country's best was a truly incredible feat. All credit too to David O'Leary and his brilliant young Leeds side. Unfortunately some of his players tired towards the end of the season, but they will benefit from the experience - as will David - and they will be even stronger for their exploits. What potential they have.

Q is for

Niall QUINN
who brilliantly supported Kevin Phillips and must take an awful lot of credit for a number of the former Watford striker's 30-goal haul. Not only that but the giant Republic of Ireland striker helped himself to some wonderful goals too and, in the process, proved to a lot of people that he is not just a target man with aerial power. For a big man he has more skill than some credit him.

Barry QUINN
who came through the youth ranks at Coventry and made an impressive first team debut for City at Old Trafford last season. Having captained the Republic of Ireland's Under-18 World Championship-winning side in 1998, he progressed to the Under-21s and made his full international debut in 2000. A big future looks assured.

R is for

Joe ROYLE
who led Manchester City back to the promised land of the FA Carling Premiership to guarantee himself god-like status at Maine Road. To win two successive promotions with a useful rather than an outstanding squad is a fantastic achievement, although it might be a while yet before Big Joe is challenging Sir Alex for the title 'King of Manchester'.

ANDY GRAY SAYS Congratulations to Manchester City; the Premiership is an even better place for the presence of such a massive club. Well done to Joe Royle too because he fully deserved his moment of glory after the Blackburn game last season. Joe is a canny manager who knows how to get the most out of whatever is at his disposal. He has the advantage of having been there before with Everton during some of their bad times and he knows all about the nitty gritty of staying up. He might not have the best squad in the Premiership but he will certainly get the best out of his players.

S is for

Alan SHEARER
who rediscovered the lethal form of old within weeks of the arrival of former England boss Bobby Robson at St James'. He clocked up the 300th goal of his career last season, and must rank up there with the great goalscorers of English football. Surprised everyone towards the end of the campaign by announcing he would retire from international football after the European Championships.

Paul SCHOLES
who is arguably one of the most complete midfield players in the country. Tenacious, skilful and with the ability to score wonderful goals from all ranges and angles, the ginger ninja is as important to Manchester United as David Beckham and Roy Keane and is equally influential on the international stage - as he proved with a number of vital goals in England's stuttering European Championship qualifying campaign - and again in the finals themselves.

T is for

Peter THORNE
who fired Stoke City to the promotion play-offs by scoring 15 goals in the club's last 13 League games. He finished the campaign with 25 goals in total, but still ended the season disappointed after Stoke lost to Gillingham in the Play-Off semis. But he did taste glory in the Auto Windscreens Shield when he scored in Stoke's 2-1 win over Bristol City in the Final at Wembley.

ZONE

U is for

David UNSWORTH

who returned to his favourite club Everton in 1998 after a couple of abortive moves to West Ham and then Aston Villa. Now he's back to his powerful, dominant best in an Everton side which also made great strides in the right direction last season. Strong and assured, Unsworth has been the 'baby' (even at the age of 27!) of an Everton defence which included veterans Richard Gough and Dave Watson - who are some 10 years older than David.

V is for

Ruud VAN NISTELROOY

who saw his dream move to Manchester United - and the personal fortune which went with it - shattered with the recurrence of his knee ligament injury just a couple of days after transfer talks had broken down because of his Old Trafford medical. One can only hope that the brilliant Dutchman can rediscover the fitness and form which made him the most sought after striker in Europe.

ANDY GRAY SAYS

Manchester United were once again head and shoulders above the their rivals and, once again, Dwight Yorke played an important role, although perhaps not the starring one of the previous treble-winning campaign. And, no sooner had the latest Premiership race been won, than Sir Alex Ferguson was getting ready to shell out £19 million on the Dutchman Ruud Van Nistelrooy. What an addition he would have been to United's already impressive goalscoring department. Still, even without Ruud you would be pushed to bet against The Reds being top again.

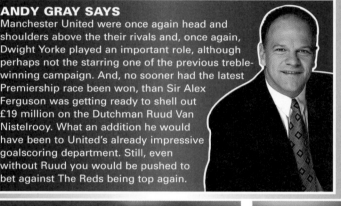

W is for

Ian WRIGHT

who began last season at West Ham and ended it in the claret and blue of promoted Burnley after loan spells with Nottingham Forest and Glasgow Celtic. In between times he was rapidly developing a lucrative career as a chat show host, popping up on the TV in civvies almost as much as he was spotted in a football strip. Oh yes, then there was the small matter of him being awarded the MBE.

X is for

Abel XAVIER

who joined Everton from PSV Eindhoven in September, 1999 for £1.5million and made 20 first team appearances for the Goodison Park club last season. He played his part in Portugal's 3-2 win over England at Euro 2000 - and he also showed some bottle to play in the finals with bright yellow hair!

Y is for

Dwight YORKE

who followed up a magnificent first season with Man United with another goal-laden campaign last term. His performances were not quite as spectacular and his partnership with Andy Cole not quite as telepathic, but the Trinidad and Tobago star still broke the 20-goal barrier again to make sure that Teddy Sheringham and Ole Gunnar Solskjaer were kicking their heels on the bench for long spells. And the smile was as wide as ever!

Z is for

Gianfranco ZOLA

who continued to delight the Stamford Bridge faithful with his customary box of tricks, although he did find goals a bit more difficult to come by last season as Chelsea flattered to deceive at home and abroad before ending the campaign on a high with a UEFA Cup-clinching spot as a result of their FA Cup Final defeat of Aston Villa.

SKY**SPORTS** FOOTBALL

REVIEW OF THE SEASON
1999-2000

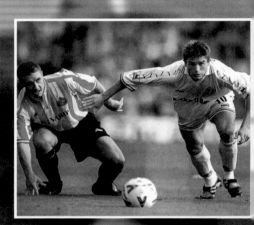

SEASON REVIEW AUGUST

QUOTES OF THE MONTH

Newcastle boss **Ruud Gullit** speaking after Alan Shearer had been sent-off by Uriah Rennie said: "I don't care if they ban or fine me. They can fine me all they like. I will still be right. The referee destroyed the game and I blame him for us losing the match."

West Ham manager **Harry Redknapp** speaking about Eyal Berkovic's defection to Celtic said: "I didn't want to sell him but once Celtic put £25,000 a week on the table he was off. Anyway, he told me he had always supported them ever since he was a kid kicking a sock around the streets of Tel Aviv!"

Magic MOMENTS

Golden Goof Award
▼ to Jaap Stam who spoiled Mark Bosnich's League debut for Man United by putting the ball past his own 'keeper in the 1-1 draw with Everton on the opening day. Not as bad as Frank Sinclair though, as the Leicester defender followed his own goal against Arsenal with another one against Chelsea.

Travel Show Award
▼ to Premiership new boys Watford who recorded a surprise away win at Liverpool. The Reds paraded £25 million worth of new talent but Tommy Mooney scored the only goal of the game to claim the unusual distinction of having scored in every division of the League in England.

Super Solo Award
▼ to Chelsea's brilliant Uruguayan Gustavo Poyet who scored two goals in the 4-0 win over Sunderland; his second a wonderful scissor-kick volley from an impudent flicked pass by Gianfranco Zola which was instantly hailed as an early contender for Goal of the Season.

PAPER TALK

Transfer deals the press assured us were dead certs but turned out to be dead losses:-

Roy Keane	Man Utd to Lazio
Robbie Fowler	Liverpool to Leeds
Robbie Keane	Wolves to Aston Villa
Tore Andre Flo	Chelsea to Newcastle
Teddy Sheringham	Man Utd to Leeds
Rivaldo	Barcelona to Man Utd
Emile Heskey	Leicester to Arsenal

AND NOW THE SKYSPORTS NEWS...

Alan Shearer was sent-off for the first time in his career, for two bookable offences, in his 100th game for Newcastle against Aston Villa. Manager Ruud Gullit, sacked soon after, went onto the pitch to confront referee Uriah Rennie after the game and had to be restrained by opposite number John Gregory.

Francis Jeffers caused a stir at Goodison Park when he slammed in a transfer request after his demands for a new £20,000 a week deal, four times his current wage, were turned down by the club. The young Everton striker, with only a handful of games to his name, later withdrew his request and apologised.

Robbie Keane completed a move from Wolves to Coventry and so became the game's most expensive teenager at £6 million. Earlier, Man United boss Alex Ferguson pulled out of the race for Keane saying he wouldn't pay more than £500,000 for the rookie striker.

SEPTEMBER SEASON REVIEW

Magic MOMENTS

Golden Goof Award

▼ to Sheffield Wednesday for what can best be described as a pathetic capitulation at St James' Park where Newcastle swaggered to their record Premiership win (8-0) with Alan Shearer hitting five and so equalling the best individual tally in a top flight match, also held by Andy Cole for Man United v Ipswich.

Giant Killing Award

▼ to First Division strugglers Oxford who, having held Everton to a 1-1 draw at the Manor Ground in the first-leg of their Worthington Cup clash, recorded a famous 1-0 win at Goodison Park - with Joey Beauchamp hitting the winner - to progress to Round Three.

Five Star Award

▼ to the Premiership's surprise side Sunderland who continued their impressive start to the season by hammering five goals past Derby whose home form was already becoming a big problem. Kevin Phillips helped himself to a Pride Park hat-trick with Gavin McCann and Niall Quinn also scoring.

QUOTES OF THE MONTH

Bayern Munich president Franz Beckenbauer, speaking about star striker **Mario Basler's** latest brush with German officialdom (fined for a late-night drinking session), said: "Players deal with their frustration in different ways. One guy will put on his training gear and go for a run in the forest; another will go to a disco."

Newcastle midfielder **Robert Lee**, speaking about his strained relationship with sacked boss Ruud Gullit, said: "He only spoke to me once in a year, and I only found out that he had axed me as captain when I saw it on the club notice board."

PAPER TALK

Transfer deals the press assured us were dead certs but turned out to be dead losses:-

Luis Enrique	Barcelona to Chelsea
Oliver Bierhoff	AC Milan to Arsenal
Mark Bosnich	Man Utd to Real Zaragoza
Roy Keane	Man Utd to Real Madrid
Tony Adams	Arsenal to Tottenham
Ruud Van Nistelrooy	PSV to Newcastle
Roberto Baggio	Inter Milan to Chelsea

AND NOW THE SKYSPORTS NEWS...

At a time when players appear to be obsessed with money it was heart-warming to hear the story of **David Tuttle** who waived the thousands of pounds Crystal Palace owed him for a signing on fee and bonuses after joining Barnsley for £125,000. He didn't want to put the cash-strapped club in even more trouble.

Kieron Dyer became an instant England hero after making a sensational 45-minute debut for his country in the 6-0 Wembley win over Luxembourg. He retired injured at half time but admitted he felt like crying as the England fans chanted 'there's only one Kieron Dyer'.

Having made a remarkable return to international action at the age of 37, **Stuart Pearce** lived up to his 'hard man' tag after suffering a broken leg only weeks into his West Ham career. 'Psycho', injured in the 1-0 win over Watford, refused a stretcher, walked off virtually unaided and then asked to go back on. Now that's hard!

ZONE

SEASON REVIEW OCTOBER

QUOTES OF THE MONTH

Arsenal's Nigerian star **Nwankwo Kanu**, speaking about being home alone in his luxury London pad, said: "I'm always stuck in the house. I'm home in the morning, home in the evening and I have nowhere to go because my family is not here with me."

Newcastle United boss **Bobby Robson**, speaking about his 'cheeky' bid for Brazilian star Ronaldo, said: "I get on well with Ronaldo and made the decision to try and sign him on loan when I heard that he was recovering from injury."

Magic MOMENTS

Golden Goof Award
▼ to nutty Brazilian Edmundo who infuriated animal lovers when he was photographed feeding beer to a monkey during a circus-style birthday party for the Vasco Da Gama player's son; imaginatively called Edmundo Junior. Hopefully, it won't be a case of 'like father, like son'.

Pie-in the-Sky Award
▼ to Spurs' David Ginola who suggested that the perennial under-achievers had set their sights on winning all three domestic trophies this season. "Our aim is to win everything," said the optimistic Frenchman. "We are going for the treble, we've had a good start and we are better than last year."

Five Star Award
▼ to Chelsea who stunned reigning English and European Champions Manchester United with a five-goal blitz at Stamford Bridge. United lost Nicky Butt, sent-off after just 23 minutes, but Chelsea were already 2-0 up and well on their way to ending United's 30-match unbeaten Premiership run.

PAPER TALK

Transfer deals the press assured us were dead certs but turned out to be dead losses:-

Roy Keane	Man Utd to Barcelona
Ronaldo	Inter Milan to Newcastle
Sol Campbell	Tottenham to Man Utd
Sol Campbell	Tottenham to Real Madrid
Mario Jardel	Porto to Leeds
Patrick Kluivert	Barcelona to Arsenal
Benito Carbone	Sheff Wed to Derby

AND NOW THE SKYSPORTS NEWS...

Coventry's **Mustapha Hadji** took physiotherapy to new extremes after natural methods to cure a foot injury failed. He amazed team-mates, not to mention the club physio, by putting two pieces of fillet steak inside his boot to protect his injured foot. Guess what? It worked- but what a smell!

No chance of **Everton** ever getting a UEFA Cup wild card by heading the Premiership Fair Play League after it was revealed

that they were the dirtiest team in the top flight having had 27 players sent-off and 442 booked since 1992.

Paul Merson, having given many vivid accounts of his life as an alcoholic and a gambler hooked on drugs, revealed in his book 'Hero and Villain: My account of a traumatic year' that he felt like killing himself when he lapsed back into drink in April, 1999. But Merse stayed dry and turned on the magic again.

NOVEMBER SEASON REVIEW

Magic MOMENTS

Super Solo Award
▼ to Marc Overmars who opened his goal account for the season with a hat-trick in the 5-1 League win over Middlesbrough; the Gunners' biggest win of the season to date. Overmars has been linked with a move to Barcelona but Arsene Wenger says he is desperate to keep the flying Dutchman.

Giant Killing Award
▼ to Rushden and Diamonds who beat Second Division Scunthorpe 2-0 in the FA Cup First Round. The Conference aristocrats, owned by Dr Martens' supremo Max Briggs, scored two second-half goals to overcome their League opponents and make a clear statement about their future ambitions.

Five Star Award
▼ to Charlton who boosted their hopes of an instant return to the Premiership by smashing five goals past Grimsby at Blundell Park. Promotion is vital for the South London club, especially as failure to do so could well result in them struggling to hang on to highly-rated boss Alan Curbishley.

QUOTES OF THE MONTH

Manchester United striker **Dwight Yorke**, speaking about how his life has changed since he became an Old Trafford celebrity, said: "My private life is always in the tabloids where I have been linked with loads of women. It hurts at first but you have to learn to live with it."

West Ham's Croatian international **Igor Stimac**, speaking about his celebrity status back home, said: "All the Croatian players are treated like heroes when we go home. The President claims we have done more for the country than all the politicians put together."

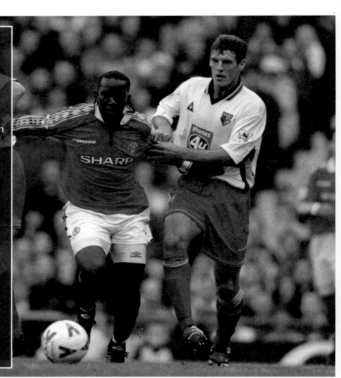

PAPER TALK

Transfer deals the press assured us were dead certs but turned out to be dead losses:-

Roy Keane	Man Utd to Celtic
Oliver Bierhoff	AC Milan to Leeds
Arsene Wenger	Arsenal to Real Madrid
Hassan Kachloul	Southampton to Liverpool
Fabrizio Ravanelli	Marseille to Tottenham
David Beckham	Man Utd to Inter Milan
Ronaldo	Inter Milan to Man Utd

AND NOW THE SKYSPORTS NEWS...

Roy Keane, who has already been linked with a host of continental clubs this season, fuelled rumours that he could quit Manchester United when his contract runs out in the summer by announcing: "As much as I love United, I am not going to sell myself short. I respect the club's position but they have to respect mine."

England qualified for the Euro 2000 finals by scraping through their Play-Off decider against Scotland after making the sudden death showdown by the skin of their teeth. **Paul Scholes** was the two-goal hero at Hampden but a Don Hutchison goal at Wembley had Kevin Keegan sweating all the way.

Newcastle's top brass revealed that veteran boss **Bobby Robson** would be offered a new, improved deal which will keep him at the club until the ripe old age of 70. Robson took a matter of weeks to lift the gloom at St James' Park after the sad reign of Ruud Gullit and is loved by all!

SEASON REVIEW DECEMBER

QUOTES OF THE MONTH

Sunderland's prolific striker **Kevin Phillips**, speaking about his ambitions for the season, said: "I would love to finish the season as the Premiership's leading scorer and win the Golden Boot in the process. It would also be a massive achievement if we could win a place in Europe."

Newcastle striker **Duncan Ferguson**, speaking about former boss Ruud Gullit's decision to drop Alan Shearer before the axe fell on him, said: "For Ruud to play anybody instead of Alan was crazy, just stupid. It just showed that the boss had lost the plot."

Magic MOMENTS

True Brit Award
▼ to Ian Wright who was awarded the MBE he will receive from the Queen at Buckingham Palace early in the year 2000. Wrighty, who has also been honoured with an appearance on 'This Is Your Life', said: "I'm so proud. Surely life cannot get any better than this."

Giant Killing Award
▼ to Second Division Burnley who inflicted the ninth home defeat of the season on Premiership strugglers Derby to take their place in the Fourth Round of the FA Cup. Andy Cooke was the goal hero for the Clarets with a 62nd minute strike which sent the travelling fans wild with delight.

Super Solo Award
▼ to Darren Ferguson, son of Sir Alex, who scored the winning goal for Wrexham in the 2-1 FA Cup Third Round defeat of Premiership big spenders Middlesbrough, to make it a painful visit to North Wales for his former Manchester United skipper Bryan Robson - and keep one Fergie in the Cup.

PAPER TALK

Transfer deals the press assured us were dead certs but turned out to be dead losses:-

Vicente Rodriguez	Velante to Arsenal
Chris Sutton	Chelsea to Tottenham
Matt Jansen	Blackburn to Rangers
Don Hutchison	Everton to Inter Milan
Hakan Sukur	Galatasaray to Leeds
Arsene Wenger	Arsenal to Japanese FA
Luis Chilavert	Velez Sarsfield to Newcastle

AND NOW THE SKYSPORTS NEWS...

Roy Keane finally ended the speculation about his future and disappointed some of Europe's biggest clubs by signing a new contract which made him the country's highest earner at £52,000 a week. He celebrated by scoring in Manchester United's 3-0 Champions League win over Valencia the same day.

Paul Gascoigne's wonder strike against Scotland at Euro 96 was voted 'The Best Goal of the 90s' in a survey carried out by MATCH magazine. Ryan Giggs' super solo goal in the FA Cup against Arsenal in 1999 came second with Michael Owen's stunner against Argentina at France 98 in third.

England, having already been drawn against age-old rivals Germany at Euro 2000, were also paired with their Italia 90 and Euro 96 tormentors for the 2002 World Cup qualifiers. Despite England's recent record against the Germans, **Kevin Keegan** reckoned there wasn't a better time to take them on.

PFA PLAYERS OF THE YEAR: 2000

Young Player
HARRY KEWELL

JANUARY SEASON REVIEW

Magic MOMENTS

Travel Show Award
▼ to Derby County, who despite playing like turkeys at home, swept aside Middlesbrough at the Riverside with young striker Malcolm Christie, who was playing non-League football little more than a year ago, making a rare start and scoring two of his side's four goals.

Giant Killing Award
▼ to First Division Tranmere who claimed their fourth Premiership scalp of the season in the two domestic Cup competitions, this time adding Sunderland to their collection thanks to a 1-0 win in the Fourth Round of the FA Cup. Mind you they had 11 players even after one was sent-off!

Super Solo Award
▼ to Liberian international striker George Weah who flew in from Milan to join the Chelsea squad for the visit of Tottenham; came off the bench after 57 minutes of the Premiership stalemate and scored the winner just half an hour into his debut for the London club.

PAPER TALK
Transfer deals the press assured us were dead certs but turned out to be dead losses:-

Gabriel Batistuta	Fiorentina to Man Utd
Geoff Horsfield	Fulham to Leeds
Nicky Butt	Man Utd to Newcastle
Kevin Phillips	Sunderland to Lazio
Duncan Ferguson	Newcastle to Derby
Matt Jansen	Blackburn to Man Utd
Taribo West	Inter Milan to West Ham

AND NOW THE SKYSPORTS NEWS...

David Beckham, sent-off in disgrace against Necaxa at the Club World Championship, was unable to attend the FIFA World Player of the Year awards to collect his runner-up prize so George Best did it on his behalf and caused a stir by saying the Manchester United midfielder wasn't as good as people seem to think.

Diego Maradona, once the greatest footballer in the world, now looks like a bloated, ageing member of the Prodigy, after being admitted to a rehab clinic to cure his recurring drug problems. At least the former Argentine skipper has got a friend in Cuban leader Fidal Castro!

Poor old **Danny Wilson** was getting it in the neck from all angles (including Parliament) as he struggled to arrest Sheffield Wednesday's fall from grace. But at least he had the full backing of his chairman Dave Richards who said: "I will never sack Danny. He is the most honest person I've worked with."

SEASON REVIEW FEBRUARY

QUOTES OF THE MONTH

Sunderland striker **Kevin Phillips**, speaking about his international prospects, said: "To play at Euro 2000 would be the pinnacle of my career. It is incredible to think that four years ago I was watching Euro 96 on the TV with my mates."

Southampton manager **Glenn Hoddle**, speaking about the public's perception of him after the England debacle, said: "If I'm considered a crank, if people want to say that I go home on a broomstick every night, maybe I'll just have to laugh about it."

Magic MOMENTS

Super Solo Award
▼ to Benito Carbone who followed up his hat-trick in Aston Villa's 3-2 FA Cup Fifth Round win over Leeds, by scoring two more in the 4-0 Premiership win at Middlesbrough. How Sheffield Wednesday miss the Italian and his wonderful box of tricks. Wembley calls for Villa.

True Brit Award
▼ to Newcastle and England skipper Alan Shearer who, having been written off in many quarters, took his goal tally for the season to 23 with two clinical strikes in the 3-0 home win over Manchester United who had Roy Keane sent-off for two bookable offences.

Five Star Award
▼ to West Ham and Bradford for serving up one of the best games of the season at Upton Park, a match which began with Hammers 'keeper Shaka Hislop suffering a broken leg after just four minutes and ended with Frank Lampard scoring a late winner to settle this 5-4 thriller.

PAPER TALK

Transfer deals the press assured us were dead certs but turned out to be dead losses:-

Ruud Van Nistelrooy	PSV to Arsenal
Jordi Cruyff	Man Utd to Liverpool
Martin O'Neill	Leicester to Celtic
Harry Kewell	Leeds to Inter Milan
Jimmy Hasselbaink	Atletico Madrid to Villa
Roberto Baggio	Inter Milan to Leeds
Rivaldo	Barcelona to Man United (again!)

AND NOW THE SKYSPORTS NEWS...

Leicester lifted the Worthington Cup thanks to two goals from free-scoring defender Matt Elliott, but he wasn't wearing the biggest smile of the day; that belonged to **Tony Cottee** who collected the first winners' medal of his 17-year career after the 2-0 win over Tranmere.

England boss **Kevin Keegan** revealed his fears about the growing number of foreign players in the English game, a seemingly irreversible trend which is making his job a nightmare. Unless there are changes Keegan says he will be forced to watch First Division football to keep tabs on potential international stars.

Glenn Hoddle was unveiled as Southampton's new 'caretaker' boss, replacing Dave Jones who was neither sacked, nor did he resign and, in another strange twist, he was offered the right to reclaim the job in a year's time after a court case he was involved in will be finished.

MARCH SEASON REVIEW

Magic MOMENTS

Super Solo Award

▼ to Jorg Albertz who scored twice in the Glasgow derby to extend Rangers' lead at the top of the Scottish Premier to 16 points. The 4-0 win was the Gers' biggest win over great rivals Celtic for 12 years and fans of the Bhoys were up in arms - again!

True Brit Award

▼ to England's promising and talented Under-21 stars who turned in a stylish display to beat a cynical Yugoslav team 3-0 to qualify for their own European Championship finals in the summer. Andy Campbell, Frank Lampard and Lee Hendrie scored the goals.

Five Star Award

▼ to Arsenal who recorded an impressive 5-1 victory in the first-leg of their UEFA Cup Fourth Round tie against Deportivo La Coruna of Spain. Frenchman Thierry Henry, the smiling version of Nicolas Anelka, enhanced his reputation with two more well taken goals.

QUOTES OF THE MONTH

Manchester United striker **Andy Cole**, speaking about his stop-start-stop international career, said: "I just don't know whether I am coming or going with England. It's getting beyond a joke."

Sunderland defender **Steve Bould**, speaking about comparisons between Kevin Phillips and Ian Wright, said: "When you watch Kev in training, he is identical to Ian. In terms of character though he's completely different. Wrighty's crackers and very loud; Kevin is very, very quiet."

PAPER TALK

Transfer deals the press assured us were dead certs but turned out to be dead losses:-

Paul Gascoigne	Middlesbrough to Brisbane
Jamie Redknapp	Liverpool to Tottenham
Nicky Weaver	Man City to Newcastle
Eyal Berkovic	Celtic to Blackburn
Don Hutchison	Everton to Leeds
Trevor Sinclair	West Ham to Arsenal
Lee Hughes	West Brom to Leicester

AND NOW THE SKYSPORTS NEWS...

The highest attendance in Premiership history - 61,592 - was recorded at Old Trafford (where else?) as **Manchester United** were held to a 1-1 draw by Liverpool, but remained unbeaten on home soil this season and on course for yet another League title.

Leeds and **Tottenham** were each fined £150,000 for the 18-man free-for-all which marred the Premiership clash between the two clubs at Elland Road in February. And the Football Association warned that clubs would be docked points for similar indiscretions in the future.

Paul Scholes and **Paolo Di Canio** went head-to-head over the same weekend in the race for the 'Goal of the Season' title as the Manchester United star brilliantly converted a David Beckham corner with a first time shot against Bradford, before the Italian scored with a stunning volley against Wimbledon. Arguments over which was the best goal quickly ensued.

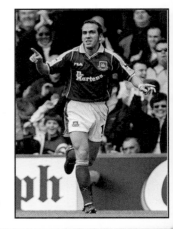

ZONE

SEASON REVIEW APRIL

QUOTES OF THE MONTH

Leeds manager **David O'Leary**, speaking about the tragic deaths of two United fans in Turkey, said: "I'm just sorry for the people who lost their lives, their families and friends. We would loved to have turned the tie around and won as a tribute to them."

Tottenham defender **Sol Campbell**, speaking about the club's seeming lack of ambition, said: "We've gone forward in little spurts but nobody is prepared to follow it through. It's like getting engaged and then having cold feet and not getting married."

Magic MOMENTS

Golden Goof Award
▼ to Manchester United's Nicky Butt and Watford's Micah Hyde who were both sent-off for their 'handbags at ten paces' scuffle in the meaningless Premiership clash at Vicarage Road between already-crowned Champions United and the already-relegated Hornets.

Travel Show Award
▼ to Ipswich Town who kept their promotion dream alive with a 3-1 win at The Valley, home of newly-crowned First Division Champions Charlton. As a result of Ipswich's victory the race for second spot went to the last day of the season with Manchester City in pole position for that runners-up place.

True Brit Award
▼ to Dion Dublin who scored the winning penalty for Aston Villa in the FA Cup Semi-Final shoot-out against Bolton just four months after a broken neck put his career on the line. Keeper David James was also a Villa hero, saving two of the Bolton spot-kicks as Villa reached their first Final since 1957.

PAPER TALK

Transfer deals the press assured us were dead certs but turned out to be dead losses:-

Michael Duberry	Leeds to Southampton
David Beckham	Man Utd to Real Madrid
Sylvain Wiltord	Bordeaux to Arsenal
Steve McManaman	Real Madrid to Leeds
Carl Cort	Wimbledon to Leicester
Eidur Gudjohnsen	Bolton to Newcastle
Christian Karembeu	Real to Liverpool

AND NOW THE SKYSPORTS NEWS...

The proposed £18.5million transfer of **Ruud Van Nistelrooy** from PSV Eindhoven to Manchester United was shelved after a row over medical tests the Dutchman refused to take. Two days later, Van Nistelrooy's dream move, indeed his career, was in tatters after damaging his fragile knee in a training ground fall.

Two **Bristol Rovers** fans were escorted from the Memorial Ground after running onto the pitch and assaulting Stoke 'keeper Gavin Ward during the 3-3 Second Division draw. Ward wrestled one of the men to the ground before team-mates waded in to protect him further.

Poor old **Stan Collymore**'s topsy-turvy career took another turn for the worst when he suffered a broken leg in a freak incident during Leicester's Premiership defeat by Derby at Pride Park. Fortunately for Stan it was forecast that he should be back in action for August.

MAY SEASON REVIEW

Magic MOMENTS

Golden Goof Award
▼ to Sheffield Wednesday who left it too late before finding some decent form - forcing a creditable draw at Arsenal after leading 3-1 - and relegation to the First Division was just about what the Owls deserved after a season of constant under-achievement. Still at least they can have a Sheffield derby now!

Super Solo Award
▼ to Rangers' midfielder Barry Ferguson who crowned a fantastic season by helping Dick Advocaat's men to yet another Championship triumph before helping himself to the Scottish Football Writers' Player of the Year award. Celtic's Mark Viduka collected the Players' Player title.

True Grit Award
▼ to George Burley and his Ipswich Town team who finally fought their way through the Play-Offs and back to the promised land of the Premiership at the fourth time of asking. Surely no-one can begrudge them their thrilling Wembley victory over Barnsley after so many near-misses?

Nationwide
DIVISION 1 PLAY-OFF WINNERS

QUOTES OF THE MONTH

Roberto Di Matteo, speaking about his winning goal against Aston Villa in the last FA Cup Final to be staged at Wembley, said: "I love Wembley - it is a great place for me and a great place for Chelsea."

Nicolas Anelka, speaking about a difficult year in Spain before helping Real Madrid clinch the Champions League, said: "If the players at Real supplied me like the players at Arsenal did then I would score more goals."

PAPER TALK
Transfer deals the press assured us were dead certs but turned out to be dead losses:-

Kevin Phillips	Sunderland to Leeds
Jordi Cruyff	Man Utd to Leicester
Lilian Thuram	Parma to Man United
David Thompson	Liverpool to Man City
Luis Enrique	Barcelona to Newcastle
Pierre Van Hooijdonk	Arnhem to Celtic
David O'Leary	Leeds to Celtic

AND NOW THE SKYSPORTS NEWS...

Manchester United were named World Team of the Year at the inaugural Laureus Sports Awards in Monaco, beating off the challenge of Australia's Rugby League World Cup winners and the USA women's soccer team which lifted the World Cup on home soil in 1999.

England skipper **Alan Shearer** announced that he would be quitting international football after the European Championships so he could devote more time and effort to both playing for Newcastle United and being with his family.

Wimbledon's love affair with the Premiership finally came to an end as the Dons perished whilst Bradford staged a dramatic, late fight to beat the drop. The Wimbledon players blamed manager Egil Olsen whilst striker Efan Ekoku blamed former owner Sam Hammam for leaving the club in the lurch. Will that famous Crazy Gang spirit ever be seen again?

HOW THEY FINISHED 1999/2000

FA Carling PREMIERSHIP

		P	W	D	L	F	A	Pts
1.	Man Utd	38	28	7	3	97	45	91
2.	Arsenal	38	22	7	9	73	43	73
3.	Leeds	38	21	6	11	58	43	69
4.	Liverpool	38	19	10	9	51	30	67
5.	Chelsea	38	18	11	9	53	34	65
6.	Aston Villa	38	15	13	10	46	35	58
7.	Sunderland	38	16	10	12	57	56	58
8.	Leicester	38	16	7	15	55	55	55
9.	West Ham	38	15	10	13	52	53	55
10.	Tottenham	38	15	8	15	57	49	53
11.	Newcastle	38	14	10	14	63	54	52
12.	Middlesbrough	38	14	10	14	46	52	52
13.	Everton	38	12	14	12	59	49	50
14.	Coventry	38	12	8	18	47	54	44
15.	Southampton	38	12	8	18	45	62	44
16.	Derby	38	9	11	18	44	57	38
17.	Bradford	38	9	9	20	38	68	36
18.	Wimbledon	38	7	12	19	46	74	33
19.	Sheff Wed	38	8	7	23	38	70	31
20.	Watford	38	6	6	26	35	77	24

Division ONE

		P	W	D	L	F	A	Pts
1.	Charlton	46	27	10	9	79	45	91
2.	Man City	46	26	11	9	78	40	89
3.	Ipswich	46	25	12	9	71	42	87
4.	Barnsley	46	24	10	12	88	67	82
5.	Birmingham	46	22	11	13	65	44	77
6.	Bolton	46	21	13	12	69	50	76
7.	Wolves	46	21	11	14	64	48	74
8.	Huddersfield	46	21	11	14	62	49	74
9.	Fulham	46	17	16	13	49	41	67
10.	QPR	46	16	18	12	62	53	66
11.	Blackburn	46	15	17	14	55	51	62
12.	Norwich	46	14	15	17	45	50	57
13.	Tranmere	46	15	12	19	57	68	57
14.	Nottm For	46	14	14	18	53	55	56
15.	C.Palace	46	13	15	18	57	67	54
16.	Sheff Utd	46	13	15	18	59	71	54
17.	Stockport	46	13	15	18	55	67	54
18.	Portsmouth	46	13	12	21	55	66	51
19.	Crewe	46	14	9	23	46	67	51
20.	Grimsby	46	13	12	21	41	67	51
21.	West Brom	46	10	19	17	43	60	49
22.	Walsall	46	11	13	22	52	77	46
23.	Port Vale	46	7	15	24	48	69	36
24.	Swindon	46	8	12	26	38	77	36

Scottish PREMIER

		P	W	D	L	F	A	Pts
1.	Rangers	36	28	6	2	96	26	90
2.	Celtic	36	21	6	9	90	38	69
3.	Hearts	36	15	9	12	47	40	54
4.	Motherwell	36	14	10	12	49	63	52
5.	St Johnstone	36	10	12	14	36	44	42
6.	Hibernian	36	10	11	15	49	61	41
7.	Dundee	36	12	5	19	45	64	41
8.	Dundee Utd	36	11	6	19	34	57	39
9.	Kilmarnock	36	8	13	15	38	52	37
10.	Aberdeen	36	9	6	21	44	83	33

Scottish DIVISION ONE

		P	W	D	L	F	A	Pts
1.	St Mirren	36	23	7	6	75	39	76
2.	Dunfermline	36	20	11	5	66	33	71
3.	Falkirk	36	20	8	8	67	40	68
4.	Livingston	36	19	7	10	60	45	64
5.	Raith	36	17	8	11	55	40	59
6.	Inverness	36	13	10	13	60	55	49
7.	Ayr	36	10	8	18	42	52	38
8.	Morton	36	10	6	20	45	61	36
9.	Airdrie	36	7	8	21	29	69	29
10.	Clydebank	36	1	7	28	17	82	10

Division TWO

		P	W	D	L	F	A	Pts
1.	Preston	46	28	11	7	74	37	95
2.	Burnley	46	25	13	8	69	47	88
3.	Gillingham	46	25	10	11	79	48	85
4.	Wigan	46	22	17	7	72	38	83
5.	Millwall	46	23	13	10	76	50	82
6.	Stoke	46	23	13	10	68	42	82
7.	Bristol Rvrs	46	23	11	12	69	45	80
8.	Notts Co	46	18	11	17	61	55	65
9.	Bristol City	46	15	19	12	59	57	64
10.	Reading	46	16	14	16	57	63	62
11.	Wrexham	46	17	11	18	52	61	62
12.	Wycombe	46	16	13	17	56	53	61
13.	Luton	46	17	10	19	61	65	61
14.	Oldham	46	16	12	18	50	55	60
15.	Bury	46	13	18	15	61	64	57
16.	Bournemouth	46	16	9	21	59	62	57
17.	Brentford	46	13	13	20	47	61	52
18.	Colchester	46	14	10	22	59	82	52
19.	Cambridge	46	12	12	22	64	65	48
20.	Oxford	46	12	9	25	43	73	45
21.	Cardiff	46	9	17	20	45	67	44
22.	Blackpool	46	8	17	21	49	77	41
23.	Scunthorpe	46	9	12	25	40	74	39
24.	Chesterfield	46	7	15	24	34	63	36

Division THREE

		P	W	D	L	F	A	Pts
1.	Swansea	46	24	13	9	51	30	85
2.	Rotherham	46	24	12	10	72	36	84
3.	Northampton	46	25	7	14	63	45	82
4.	Darlington	46	21	16	9	66	36	79
5.	Peterborough	46	22	12	12	63	54	78
6.	Barnet	46	21	12	13	59	53	75
7.	Hartlepool	46	21	9	16	60	49	72
8.	Cheltenham	46	20	10	16	50	42	70
9.	Torquay	46	19	12	15	62	52	69
10.	Rochdale	46	18	14	14	57	54	68
11.	Brighton	46	17	16	13	64	46	67
12.	Plymouth	46	16	18	12	55	51	66
13.	Macclesfield	46	18	11	17	66	61	65
14.	Hull	46	15	14	17	43	43	59
15.	Lincoln	46	15	14	17	67	69	59
16.	Southend	46	15	11	20	53	61	56
17.	Mansfield	46	16	8	22	50	65	56
18.	Halifax	46	15	9	22	44	58	54
19.	L.Orient	46	13	13	20	47	52	52
20.	York	46	12	16	18	39	53	52
21.	Exeter	46	11	11	24	46	72	44
22.	Shrewsbury	46	9	13	24	40	67	40
23.	Carlisle	46	9	12	25	42	75	39
24.	Chester	46	10	9	27	44	79	39

Scottish DIVISION TWO

		P	W	D	L	F	A	Pts
1.	Clyde	36	18	11	7	65	37	65
2.	Alloa	36	17	13	6	58	38	64
3.	Ross County	36	18	8	10	57	39	62
4.	Arbroath	36	11	14	11	52	55	47
5.	Partick	36	12	10	14	42	44	46
6.	Stranraer	36	9	18	9	47	46	45
7.	Stirling	36	11	7	18	60	72	40
8.	Stenhousemuir	36	10	8	18	44	59	38
9.	QOS	36	8	9	19	45	75	33
10.	Hamilton	36	10	14	12	39	44	29

Scottish DIVISION THREE

		P	W	D	L	F	A	Pts
1.	Queen's Park	36	20	9	7	54	37	69
2.	Berwick	36	19	9	8	53	30	66
3.	Forfar	36	17	10	9	64	40	61
4.	East Fife	36	17	8	11	45	39	59
5.	Cowdenbeath	36	15	9	12	59	43	54
6.	Dumbarton	36	15	8	13	53	51	53
7.	East Stirling	36	11	7	18	28	50	40
8.	Brechin	36	10	8	18	42	51	38
9.	Montrose	36	10	7	19	39	54	37
10.	Albion	36	5	7	24	33	75	22

Please sir, Mr Robson, I've cut my foot!

STRANGE WAYS to get injured

Dave Beasant: Dropped a bottle of salad cream on his foot. Hardly a great advert for his goalkeeping skills, eh?

James Beattie: Slipped on a flip-flop - beats banana skins, we suppose.

Dean Barrick: A waitress tipped a cup of coffee into his lap and scalded the inside of his thighs.

Alan Mullery: Put his back out shaving. What he was shaving is anybody's guess.

Steve Howey: Caught his foot in a rabbit hole on a training run.

Richard Edghill: Injured his groin on his fireplace after a fall down the stairs. Honest!

Kevin Keegan: Missed a couple of matches after getting a toe stuck in a bath tap.

Charles 'Chic' Brodie: Brentford goalkeeper injured knee ligaments when a dog ran into him during a game.

John Durnin: Crashed his golf buggy during a round.

Alan Shearer: Almost sliced three of his toes off running through broken glass - naked!

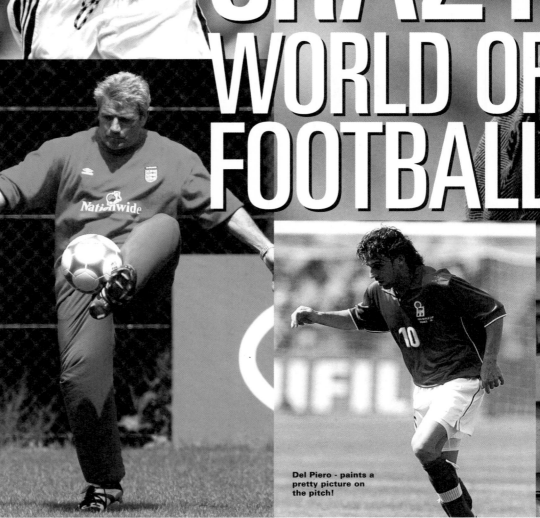

CRAZY WORLD OF FOOTBALL

KEVIN KEEGAN QUOTES apparently!

England have the best fans in the world and Scotland's are second-to-none.

It's like a toaster, the ref's shirt pocket - every time there's a tackle, up pops a yellow card.

England can end the millennium as it started - as the greatest football nation in the world.

You can't do better than go away from home and draw.

He's using his strength and that is his strength, his strength.

Gary always weighed up his options, especially when he had no choice.

The tide is very much in our court now.

Chile have three options - they could win or lose.

I came to Nantes two-years-ago and it's much the same today, except that it's totally different.

In some ways, cramp is worse than having a broken leg.

Del Piero - paints a pretty picture on the pitch!

Glass

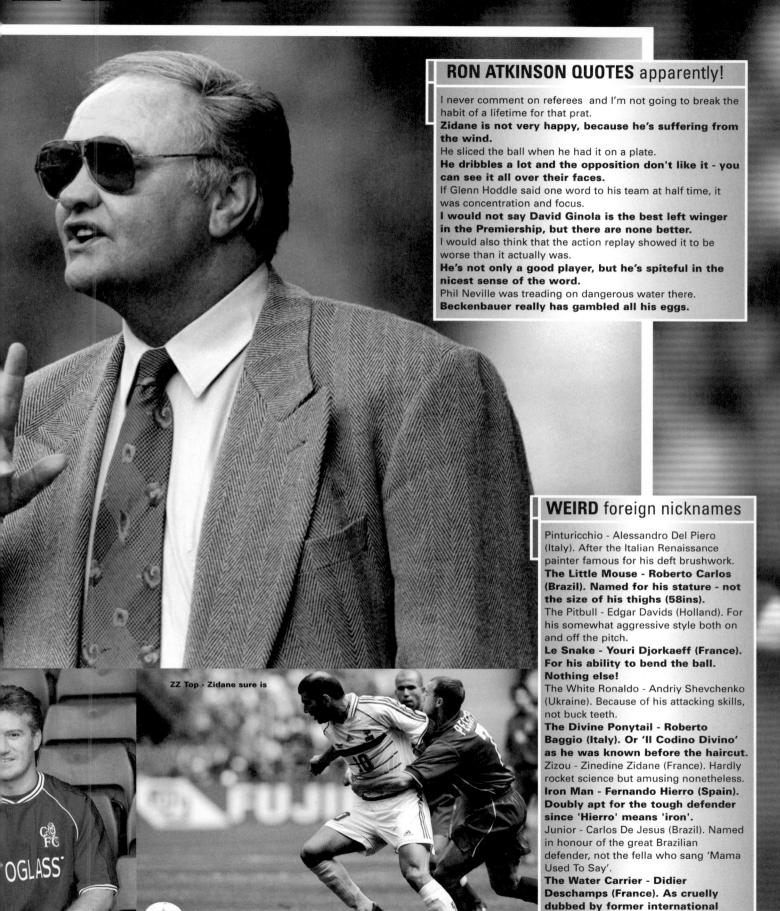

RON ATKINSON QUOTES apparently!

I never comment on referees and I'm not going to break the habit of a lifetime for that prat.

Zidane is not very happy, because he's suffering from the wind.

He sliced the ball when he had it on a plate.

He dribbles a lot and the opposition don't like it - you can see it all over their faces.

If Glenn Hoddle said one word to his team at half time, it was concentration and focus.

I would not say David Ginola is the best left winger in the Premiership, but there are none better.

I would also think that the action replay showed it to be worse than it actually was.

He's not only a good player, but he's spiteful in the nicest sense of the word.

Phil Neville was treading on dangerous water there.

Beckenbauer really has gambled all his eggs.

WEIRD foreign nicknames

Pinturicchio - Alessandro Del Piero (Italy). After the Italian Renaissance painter famous for his deft brushwork.

The Little Mouse - Roberto Carlos (Brazil). Named for his stature - not the size of his thighs (58ins).

The Pitbull - Edgar Davids (Holland). For his somewhat aggressive style both on and off the pitch.

Le Snake - Youri Djorkaeff (France). For his ability to bend the ball. Nothing else!

The White Ronaldo - Andriy Shevchenko (Ukraine). Because of his attacking skills, not buck teeth.

The Divine Ponytail - Roberto Baggio (Italy). Or 'Il Codino Divino' as he was known before the haircut.

Zizou - Zinedine Zidane (France). Hardly rocket science but amusing nonetheless.

Iron Man - Fernando Hierro (Spain). Doubly apt for the tough defender since 'Hierro' means 'iron'.

Junior - Carlos De Jesus (Brazil). Named in honour of the great Brazilian defender, not the fella who sang 'Mama Used To Say'.

The Water Carrier - Didier Deschamps (France). As cruelly dubbed by former international team-mate Eric Cantona.

ZZ Top - Zidane sure is

AND HOLDSWORTH MUST SCORE

BOLTON STRIKER DEAN RELIVES HIS WEMBLEY NIGHTMARE... AND WE RELIVE A FEW OTHERS

BOLTON STRIKER Dean Holdsworth is such a nice guy that he'll probably forgive us for reminding him of the moment he must have wanted Wembley's famous pitch to open up and swallow him whole.

Well, he probably won't, but we're going to anyway because, just as we toast triumphs of an extraordinary nature, football followers also love to gloat when it all goes horribly wrong.

While Bolton fans are probably already cringing in their seats as they read this, Aston Villa supporters will no doubt still be beaming from ear to ear as they recall the moment Deano's dream turned into a living nightmare.

The former Wimbledon striker, like so many Wembley wobblers before him, was guilty of an incredible miss during the FA Cup Semi-Final clash

with Villa beneath the Twin Towers last April.

A virtually open goal opportunity minutes from time would, had it been converted, put Bolton in the FA Cup Final for the first time in 32 years.

The chance went begging, Dean held his head in his hands and Villa went on to win on penalties.

To his credit, the distraught striker recovered his composure in time to score from the spot in the shoot-out and he later pledged that glaring miss would not affect him. Well, after a time anyway.

He admitted at the time: "That miss will haunt me for a while, but it won't take me a long time to get over it. I'm a strong character."

Good job really, because not too many weeks later there was more

disappointment for Dean and his Bolton team-mates as they lost in the promotion Play-Off Semi-Finals to Ipswich.

But, anyway Dean, let's get back to that miss. Just what happened?

"If anything I hit the ball too well," he said. "There were two people on the line and I knew I had to get a good connection, the ball went over the bar.

"It was my biggest disappointment in football, especially as we had done ourselves so proud against a top six side in the Premier League who we more than matched.

"I went out there and played my heart out. I couldn't have done anymore and on another day the chances would have gone in. I will bounce back. I've got to."

We hope he's right.

ZONE

Crunch - there goes
Gazza's career

That Aldo nicely - for
Wimbledon that is

Gary bitter - Mabbutt's
own goal gives
Coventry the Cup

10 more WEMBLEY DISASTERS

PAUL GASCOIGNE: Tottenham v Nottingham Forest, 1991 – Gazza's crazy tackle effectively wrecked his career.

GORDON SMITH: Brighton v Man Utd, 1983 – where the phrase 'And Smith must score…' came from. Now the title of a Brighton fanzine.

GARETH SOUTHGATE: England v Germany, 1996 – does anyone need reminding about THAT penalty miss?

JOHN ALDRIDGE: Liverpool v Wimbledon, 1988 – famous penalty miss cost the Reds dear.

KEVIN MORAN: Man Utd v Everton, 1985 – the first player to be sent-off in an FA Cup Final. And he wasn't allowed to get his medal.

GARY MABBUTT: Tottenham v Coventry, 1987 – sickening own goal handed Coventry the Cup.

NORMAN HUNTER/PETER SHILTON: England v Poland, 1973 – who was really 'The Clown' on THAT night?

STEWART KENNEDY: Scotland v England, 1975 – reputation of dodgy Scottish 'keepers still in tact after England's 5-1 win.

TOMMY HUTCHISON: Man City v Tottenham, 1981 – a goal at each end for The Hutch in a Cup Final stalemate.

DAVID JAMES: Aston Villa v Chelsea, 2000 – the Villa 'keeper handed Chelsea the FA Cup, literally - spilling the ball to Roberto Di Matteo.

LAST FEBRUARY Kirsty Gallacher beat off competition from other soccer sirens to be voted as the TV sports personality men would most like to take on a Valentine's date.

And if further proof that Sky Sports has the top telly totty was needed, Soccer AM's Helen Chamberlain and presenter Kelly Dalglish also appeared in the top three.

Kirsty, a presenter on Sky Sports.comTV, won 45% of the vote ahead of Helen (21%). She was reported as saying at the time: "I'd like to offer a Valentine's kiss to every football fan who voted for me." Allegedly.

Probably more realistically she also said: "I am delighted to have been thought of as an ideal Valentine's date. I can only thank all those fans who took the time to take part." Apparently!

Either way, you have to agree that Kirsty, a nominee for Best Newcomer at the inaugural Royal Television Society Sports Awards in 1999, is a welcome sight on our screens. Especially when you've just been watching an interview with Martin Keown or Peter Beardsley!

Kirsty's father, golfer Bernard Gallacher, was Europe's Ryder Cup captain in 1997.

VALENTINE POLL RESULT

1	Kirsty Gallacher	(45%)
2	Helen Chamberlain	(21%)
3	Kelly Dalglish	(10%)
4	Gabby Yorath	(7%)
5	Kate Hoey	(6%)*
6	Karren Brady	(5%)
7	Carrie Frais	(1%)
8	Claire Tomlinson	(1%)

*Not sure if this vote is to be taken too seriously

GIRLS ON
KIRSTY IS TOP TELLY TOTT

KARREN BRADY   KATE HOEY

KELLY DALGLISH

CLARE TOMLINSON

HELEN CHAMBERLAIN

Sky's GOLDEN GIRLS

KELLY DALGLISH

Kelly Dalglish is a presenter on Sky Sports.comTV - the 24 hour sports news channel on Sky Digital. She joined the Sky Sports.comTV team at the channel's launch in August 1998. She presents the early morning programme Good Morning Sports Fans with co-presenters who include Mike Wedderburn and Rhodri Williams. Born in Glasgow in 1976, Kelly – as everyone now knows - is the daughter of Scottish football legend Kenny Dalglish. Kelly joined Sky Sports.comTV after completing a four-year Maths degree at Glasgow University.

KIRSTY GALLACHER

Kirsty Gallacher is also a presenter on Sky Sports.comTV. She worked behind-the-scenes at Sky Sports for two years starting as a production junior before progressing to editorial assistant. She has also worked on the production of Sky's coverage of the European and US PGA Tours including Europe's success in the 1997 Ryder Cup at Valderrama. Following a screen test, Kirsty was offered a three-year contract with Sky Sports. During this time she has become a well-known face to viewers as a presenter on the flagship sports news programme, Sky Sports Centre and on Sky Sports.comTV.

CLARE TOMLINSON

Clare is a presenter on Sky Sports Centre, the evening sports news bulletin on Sky digital. She also presents Goals on Sunday, the weekly review of Saturday's Premiership programme. Clare - who joined Sky Sports in 1998 - spent six years working on the other side of the camera in media relations, including a spell at the Football Association. She experienced the euphoria of Euro 96 while based at Burnham Beaches with the England squad. Before joining Sky Sports Clare spent two years setting up and heading the Communications Department at Arsenal Football Club.

HELEN CHAMBERLAIN

Helen is the glamorous half of the Soccer AM double-act, sharing the spotlight with co-host Tim Lovejoy. Her dedication to Torquay United knows no bounds and she rarely misses a chance to see her team in action. Helen joined Sky in 1995 after a diverse career as a Blue Coat at Pontins, a disc jockey and a public entertainer at Chessington World of Adventures in 1993 where for two seasons she was a public entertainer. After a spell as a presenter on Nickelodoen she was subsequently recruited by Sky to present the popular Saturday morning football show.

GIVE US A CLUE

We've given you three clues to the identity of 20 players or managers from the English and Scottish leagues. If you name the player in question after the first clue award yourself 10 points; if you name him after two award yourself 5 points; or after three clues award yourself 1 point. There's a maximum of 200 points at stake so see how you get on. Are you a football champ or chump?

STAR 1 [ ] POINTS

At the start of last season I was playing for West Ham
I had loan spells with Nottingham Forest and Celtic
I finished the season at Burnley

STAR 2 [ ] POINTS

I'm called Lurch and began my League career with Wimbledon
I was a hero in the 1988 FA Cup Final - but didn't score a goal
Last season I was playing for Nottingham Forest

STAR 3 [ ] POINTS

I was a prolific goalscorer for Liverpool
I played international football for the Republic of Ireland
I am now the manager of Tranmere

STAR 4 [ ] POINTS

I played almost 300 League games for Charlton, scoring 59 goals
Newcastle is the only other club I have played for
Ruud Gullit made me an outcast before he was sacked

STAR 5 [ ] POINTS

I played for England schoolboys but became a full international with Wales
My father was a well-known Rugby League player
I was hailed as the new George Best

STAR 6 [ ] POINTS

I came from Barnet but Wimbledon gave me League football
I was a Play-Off Final winner at Wembley last season
Barry Fry is my manager

STAR 7 [ ] POINTS

I began my career with Liverpool but didn't make a first team appearance
I played 137 League games for Wigan
I helped keep Bradford in the Premiership last season but now I am in charge of a First Division side.

STAR 8 [ ] POINTS

I skippered the World Cup winners in 1998
I have won the European Cup with two different teams
Eric Cantona once described me as 'a water carrier'

STAR 20 — POINTS
My father is a well-respected manager
I began my career with Bournemouth
I am married to a famous singer

STAR 19 — POINTS
I started my career as a goalkeeper with Bristol Rovers
But made my name with Crystal Palace
I was in England's Euro 2000 squad last summer

STAR 18 — POINTS
I was born in Bermuda
I helped Manchester City win promotion last season
I am called 'The Goat'

STAR 17 — POINTS
I finished my playing career with Aberdeen last season
I had a long spell with Manchester United
I was badly injured in my last ever game

STAR 16 — POINTS
I quit playing football last season and now I'm a pro golfer
I began my playing career with Birmingham
I had two spells with West Ham either side of a move to Liverpool

STAR 15 — POINTS
I played for Croatia Sydney in Australia
My first English club was Aston Villa
I won a Premiership medal last season

STAR 14 — POINTS
I had two spells as a player with the Premiership team I now manage
We have won promotion twice in three seasons
We play at The Valley

STAR 13 — POINTS
I was a Premiership title winner with Blackburn
Alan Shearer was my strike partner
I was sold by Rovers for £10 million

STAR 12 — POINTS
I was rejected by Southampton as a kid
I made my name at Watford
I was the Premiership's leading scorer last season

STAR 11 — POINTS
I am known in Scotland as 'The Hammer'
I hail from Germany
I won a Scottish Premiership medal last season

STAR 9 — POINTS
I am an England Under-21 international at Upton Park
I share the same surname with a top Premiership striker
I broke my leg playing for West Ham last season

STAR 10 — POINTS
I started my career with York City before joining Sunderland
I was once a £1 million striker
I just missed out on promotion with Darlington last season

NATIONWIDE PHOTO TRIBUTE

FIRST DIVISION
CHAMPIONS: CHARLTON

'WE'RE GOING

PHOTO SPECIAL ON THE TEAMS WHO ENJOYED TH

GLANDEN MOTORS
01772-735811

ALSO PROMOTED:
MANCHESTER CITY

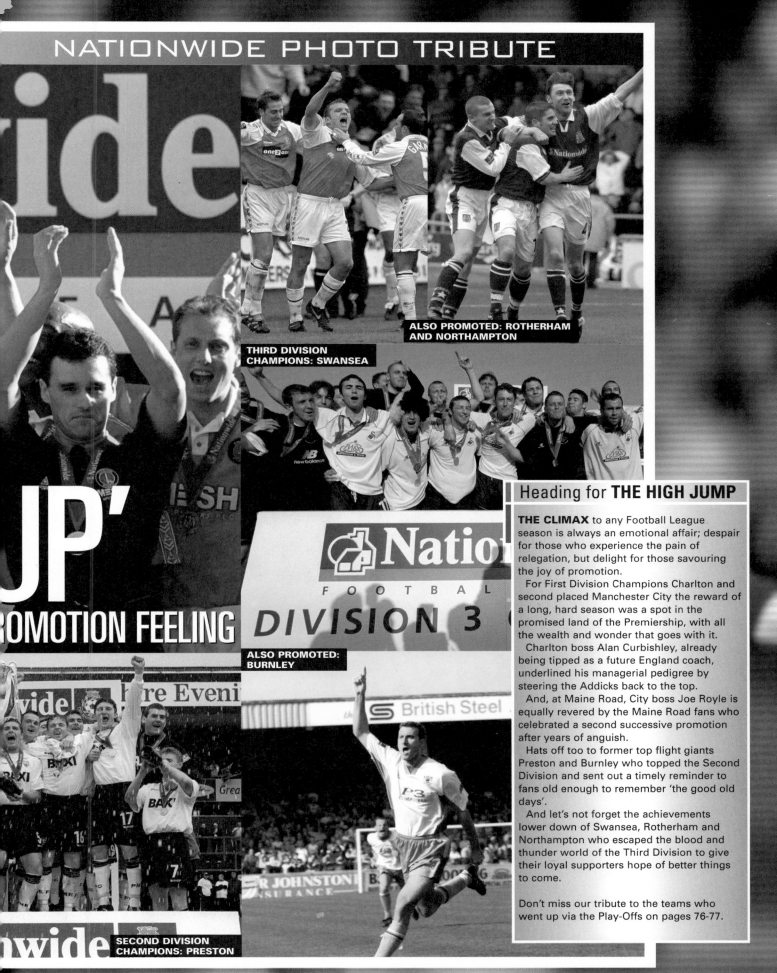

NATIONWIDE PHOTO TRIBUTE

ALSO PROMOTED: ROTHERHAM AND NORTHAMPTON

THIRD DIVISION CHAMPIONS: SWANSEA

ALSO PROMOTED: BURNLEY

SECOND DIVISION CHAMPIONS: PRESTON

Heading for THE HIGH JUMP

THE CLIMAX to any Football League season is always an emotional affair; despair for those who experience the pain of relegation, but delight for those savouring the joy of promotion.

For First Division Champions Charlton and second placed Manchester City the reward of a long, hard season was a spot in the promised land of the Premiership, with all the wealth and wonder that goes with it.

Charlton boss Alan Curbishley, already being tipped as a future England coach, underlined his managerial pedigree by steering the Addicks back to the top.

And, at Maine Road, City boss Joe Royle is equally revered by the Maine Road fans who celebrated a second successive promotion after years of anguish.

Hats off too to former top flight giants Preston and Burnley who topped the Second Division and sent out a timely reminder to fans old enough to remember 'the good old days'.

And let's not forget the achievements lower down of Swansea, Rotherham and Northampton who escaped the blood and thunder world of the Third Division to give their loyal supporters hope of better things to come.

Don't miss our tribute to the teams who went up via the Play-Offs on pages 76-77.

SKY SPORTS NATIONWIDE REVIEW

ANDY HUNT

Division ONE

TOP LEAGUE SCORERS

Andy Hunt	Charlton 24
Shaun Goater	Manchester City 23
David Johnson	Ipswich 22
Craig Hignett	Barnsley 19
Iwan Roberts	Norwich City 17

MOST RED CARDS (all two)

Mike Whitlow	Bolton
Paul Warhurst	Bolton
Nigel Quashie	Nottingham Forest
Fitzroy Simpson	Portsmouth
Chris Kiwomya	QPR
Clint Hill	Tranmere
Gareth Roberts	Tranmere
Jimmy Walker	Walsall
Larus Sigurdsson	West Brom
Matt Carbon	West Brom

Most goals scored	Barnsley 88
Least goals scored	Swindon 38
Least goals conceded	Manchester City 40
Most goals conceded	Walsall/ Swindon 77
Most draws	West Brom 19
Highest crowd	Man City v H'dersfield: 32,936

PFA TEAM OF THE YEAR

Richard Wright (Ipswich); **Gary Rowett** (Birmingham); **Richard Rufus** (Charlton); **Chris Coleman** (Fulham); **Chris Powell** (Charlton); **John Robinson** (Charlton); **Mark Kinsella** (Charlton); **Craig Hignett** (Barnsley); **Mark Kennedy** (Manchester City); **Andy Hunt** (Charlton); **Marcus Stewart** (Huddersfield/Ipswich)

Division TWO

TOP LEAGUE SCORERS

Andy Payton	Burnley 2
Neil Harris	Millwall 2
Peter Thorne	Stoke City 2
Sean Devine	Wycombe 2
Jamie Cureton	Bristol Rovers 2
Jason Roberts	Bristol Rovers 2
Jonathan Macken	Preston 1

RED CARDS (all two)

Russell Perrett	Cardiff Ci
Ricky Newman	Millwa
Phil Hardy	Wrexha
Jason Cousins	Wycomb

Most goals scored	Gillingham 1
Least goals scored	Chesterfield 3
Least goals conceded	Preston 3
Most goals conceded	Colchester 8
Most draws	Bristol City 1
Highest crowd	Burnley v Preston: 22,3

PFA TEAM OF THE YEAR

Roy Carroll (Wigan); **Graham Alexander** (Preston); **Steve Davis** (Burnley); **Michael Jackson** (Preston); **Mickey Bell** (Bristol City); **Glen Little** (Burnley); **Sean Gregan** (Preston); **Darren Caskey** (Reading); **Graham Kavanagh** (Stoke City); **Jason Roberts** (Brist Rovers); **Jonathan Macken** (Preston)

STATS ROUND-UP

SKY SPORTS NATIONWIDE REVIEW

ANDY PAYTON

MARCO GABBIADINI

Division THREE

TOP LEAGUE SCORERS

Marco Gabbiadini	Darlington	24
Martin Carruthers	Southend	19
Leo Fortune-West	Rotherham	17
Gary Alexander	Exeter	16
John Askey	Macclesfield	16
Richie Barker	Macclesfield	16
Tony Bedeau	Torquay	16

MOST RED CARDS (all two)

Mark Arber	Barnet
Stuart Whitehead	Carlisle
Darren Moss	Chester
Gary Strodder	Hartlepool
Nathan Jones	Southend
Kevin Hulme	York

Most goals scored	Rotherham 72
Least goals scored	York 39
Most goals conceded	Exeter 72
Least goals conceded	Swansea 30
Most Draws	Plymouth 18
Highest crowd	Plymouth v Torquay: 14,893

PFA TEAM OF THE YEAR

Mike Pollitt (Rotherham); **Ian Hendon** (Northampton); **Matt Bound** (Swansea City); **Craig Liddle** (Darlington); **Matt Lockwood** (Leyton Orient); **Darren Currie** (Barnet); **Tommy Miller** (Hartlepool); **Neil Heaney** (Darlington); **Nick Cusack** (Swansea); **Marco Gabbadini** (Darlington); **Richie Barker** (Macclesfield)

ALL THE FACTS OF THE NATIONWIDE LEAGUE: 1999-2000

NATIONWIDE PLAY-OFFS 2000

FIRST DIVISION PLAY-OFFS:
Ipswich 4 Barnsley 2

IPSWICH BOSS George Burley finally experienced the sweet taste of Play-Off victory at the fourth time of asking, and the Suffolk side did it in some style against Dave Bassett's Barnsley.

In each of the previous three seasons Ipswich had reached the Play-Offs and on each occasion they suffered the disappointment of defeat.

Not this time though and, having bravely disposed of Bolton in the Semis, they took their place at Wembley where goals from Tony Mowbray, Richard Naylor, Marcus Stewart and Martijn Reuser gave them a place in the Premiership.

Manager Burley singled out the performance of Richard Wright for praise before the 'keeper set off for Euro 2000 with England.

Scot Burley said: "We saw why Richard Wright is in the England squad - he is the finest young 'keeper in the country. There's no limit to how far he can go in the game and I think he could be the next Gordon Banks. He works so hard and has got the reward he deserves."

About the club's long-awaited return to the Premiership, Burley added: "As a manager, I want to be in the top flight and I want this club to be in the top flight. This has always been my club - it has been in my life for 20 years and now we can look forward to the challenge of staying with the big boys in the Premiership."

Ipswich, Gillingham and Peterborough are
WALKING IN A WEN

NATIONWIDE PLAY-OFFS 2000

SECOND DIVISION PLAY-OFFS:
Gillingham 3 Wigan 2

AFTER THE HEARTBREAK of last season's Play-Off Final, when Gillingham were cruelly denied by Manchester City in the most dramatic circumstances, the Gills got it right second time.

But, unlike the previous year's encounter with City, it was the Gills who were on a knife edge until the closing stages.

The men from Kent were trailing 2-1 with just seven minutes remaining, before headed goals from Steve Butler and Andy Thomson helped them to complete a stunning turnaround.

Gills boss Peter Taylor, who had worked for the club without a contract since taking over from Tony Pulis last summer, said he wasn't surprised to have clinched promotion, despite a tight Final which was perhaps shaded by Wigan.

He said: "I thought all season that we were good enough to get promotion.

"It's tremendous for the club, and the chairman and the supporters. As for me, it is the first thing I've ever won as a manager, apart from some good matches, so I'm delighted to have got promotion to the First Division."

THIRD DIVISION PLAY-OFFS:
Darlington 0 Peterborough 1

THERE'S CERTAINLY never a dull moment when Peterborough boss Barry Fry is around. Days after winning a nail-biting Final, he was involved in a boardroom bust-up and claimed he had been sacked whilst chairman Peter Boizot reckoned Fry had walked out.

All was settled amicably 24 hours later, however, as Fry admitted there had been a mis-understanding and that he was happy to lead Posh into the Second Division - and beyond.

Peterborough's goal hero on a wet, blustery night at Wembley was former Wimbledon striker Andy Clarke who had received the mother of all rollickings from no-nonsense Fry after an awful first half show.

"I had a few choice words at half-time and afterwards we played great and created loads of chances," said Fry. "The only disappointment was we only got one goal because that was no good for my ticker."

Goal hero Clarke added: "It was the best moment of my life. I had a bad start to the game and got a bit of a roasting in the dressing-room. But we raised our game and I was very happy with the goal I got."

BLEY WONDERLAND

RANGERS
SCOTTISH CHAMPIONS 2000

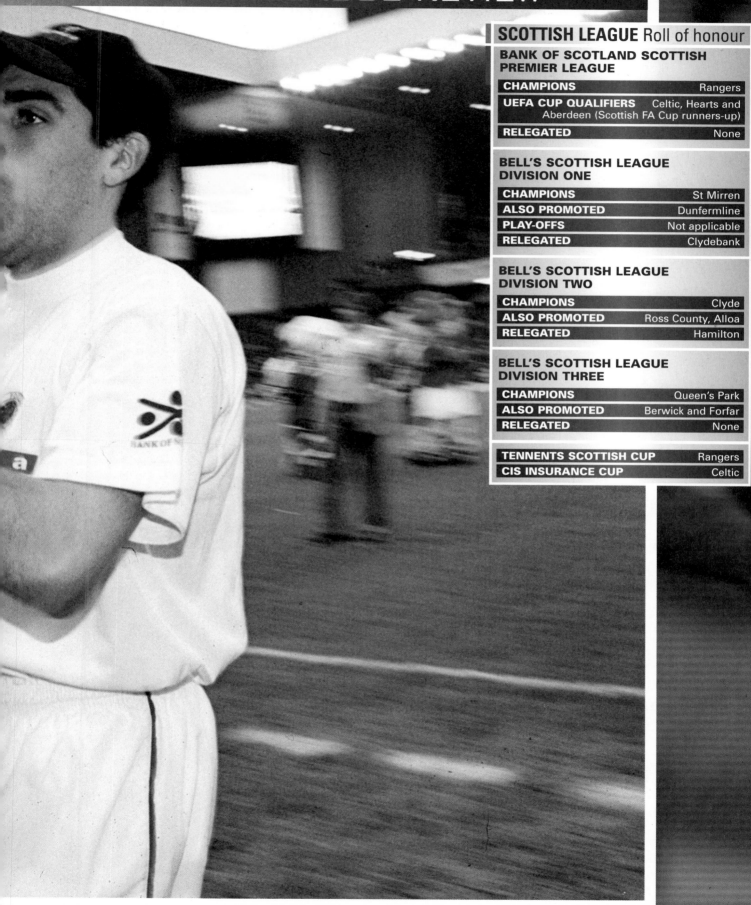

ZONE

SCOTTISH LEAGUE REVIEW

SCOTTISH LEAGUE Roll of honour

BANK OF SCOTLAND SCOTTISH PREMIER LEAGUE

CHAMPIONS	Rangers
UEFA CUP QUALIFIERS	Celtic, Hearts and Aberdeen (Scottish FA Cup runners-up)
RELEGATED	None

BELL'S SCOTTISH LEAGUE DIVISION ONE

CHAMPIONS	St Mirren
ALSO PROMOTED	Dunfermline
PLAY-OFFS	Not applicable
RELEGATED	Clydebank

BELL'S SCOTTISH LEAGUE DIVISION TWO

CHAMPIONS	Clyde
ALSO PROMOTED	Ross County, Alloa
RELEGATED	Hamilton

BELL'S SCOTTISH LEAGUE DIVISION THREE

CHAMPIONS	Queen's Park
ALSO PROMOTED	Berwick and Forfar
RELEGATED	None

TENNENTS SCOTTISH CUP	Rangers
CIS INSURANCE CUP	Celtic

GLASGOW RANGERS TRIBUTE

MACnificent!
THERE'S NO STOPPING RECORD-BREAKING RANGERS

100 not out

HAVING CANTERED to yet another Scottish League title, Rangers finished the season by setting a new world record - claiming their 100th major trophy with an easy victory in the Final of the Tennents Scottish Cup.

But their passage into the history books was somewhat tainted by the injury to Aberdeen 'keeper Jim Leighton who was carried off in the second minute of his 839th and last-ever appearance.

Dons striker Robbie Winters was forced to go in goal, because the underdogs had not selected a substitute goalkeeper, and the result after that was something of a formality.

Winters had a hard time as goals from Giovanni van Bronckhorst, Tony Vidmar, Billy Dodds and a spectacular strike from German Jorg Albertz sealed another double for the Glasgow giants.

Rangers boss Dick Advocaat said: "I was pleased with the result, but it had everything to do with the injury to Leighton. From that moment the game was over because it is difficult for an outfield player to go straight into goal.

"I feel sorry for Leighton because he has had a brilliant career and he deserved a better end than what happened in the Final."

DICK'S overseas XI

DICK ADVOCAAT made Scottish football history during the Championship-winning campaign by fielding an all-foreign starting XI, against St Johnstone.

Even though Billy Dodds, Neil McCann, Barry Nicholson and Mark Brown were all available, the Rangers boss caused a stir with his controversial starting line-up.

Amazingly, of the 11 players the Dutchman selected TEN of them came from different countries. with Klos and Albertz the only exceptions.

Advocaat's continental starting line-up read: Stefan Klos (Germany), Claudio Reyna (USA), Lorenzo Amoruso (Italy), Tony Vidmar (Australia), Arthur Numan (Holland), Andrei Kanchelskis (Russia), Giovanni Van Bronckhorst (Holland), Tugay (Turkey), Jorg Albertz (Germany), Rod Wallace (England), Seb Rozental (Chile).

GLASGOW RANGERS TRIBUTE

EUROPEAN SUCCESS must follow

IT'S OKAY dominating the Scottish Premier every season, but the true test of Rangers' character and class has to be in European competition.

So many times in the recent past they have let themselves and their fans down in Europe, although last season they did much to shake off their 'Euro flops' tag.

The Light Blues just missed out on progressing from the group stages of the Champions League and Advocaat believes European glory is not a bagpipe dream.

"I think we had an excellent campaign. We were up against some quality teams but competed well on that level. With luck and more quality, we could perhaps have gone further.

"The team is improving and we have more experience every year."

BERTZ

BARRY FERGUSON

ADVOCAAT AND FERGIE honoured

JUST AS RANGERS winning the title was no great shock, it came as no surprise when boss Dick Advocaat was named the Scottish football writers' Manager of the Year for the second consecutive season.

The Scottish Premier League Champions retained their title in style under Advocaat, ending the season with a huge winning margin over nearest rivals Celtic.

Advocaat, who also engineered a better Rangers' showing in Europe, said: "I'm very pleased with the award. I'm told it is not often you get this two years in succession so I'm honoured."

So too was young Rangers and Scotland midfielder Barry Ferguson who was named the Player of the Year - even though he thought it should have gone to one of his team-mates.

He said: "I am delighted to win this award but Giovanni van Bronckhorst and Craig Moore have been brilliant for us this year and I thought one of them would win it."

OLD FIRM CLASSICS

CELTIC v RANGERS
THE GREATEST DERBIES OF ALL?

There have been many great Glasgow derbies since the first meeting of the Old Firm back in 1891. Perhaps not all classics in terms of quality football, but for passion and commitment there's little to match a Celtic v Rangers affair. The top teams in Manchester, Liverpool and London might argue differently but, surely, Glasgow is the place to be for dynamite derbies. Here we take a look back at some of the best down the years.

March 21 1891
CELTIC 2 RANGERS 2

The very first League meeting of the Old Firm. A crowd of 12,000 packed into Parkhead to witness the historic occasion with goals from Dowds and Campbell for the home side being cancelled out by strikes from Hislop and McCreadie for Rangers. The battle lines had been drawn up.

May 6 1905
CELTIC 2 RANGERS 1

With both teams ending the season level on 41 points, and even though Celtic had a better goal difference and average, a Championship play-off took place in front of 30,000 fans at Hampden Park. Rangers, surprisingly, were favourites but Celtic got their just rewards with a 2-1 win - and went on to retain the title for the next five years.

September 10 1960
CELTIC 1 RANGERS 5

With an hour gone and Rangers leading 1-0 another tight finish was expected to a fourth derby showdown in as many weeks. But a four-goal burst by the away side inside 19 minutes left Celtic on their knees and with only a late consolation to lessen their blushes. It was the first time Celtic had conceded five goals at home for 13 years.

March 22 1986
RANGERS 4 CELTIC 4

Celtic, looking good at 3-1, suffered a setback when Willie McStay was sent-off - and Rangers took full advantage. Cammy Fraser scored twice and Robert Fleck put the home side ahead with a fortunate deflection. But Murdo MacLeod snatched a dramatic equaliser for Celtic who claimed a decisive point on their way to the title.

ZONE

OLD FIRM CLASSICS

October 17 1987
RANGERS 2 CELTIC 2

Arguably the most fiery Old Firm derby of all time reached boiling point with three players - Gers pair Chris Woods and Terry Butcher and Celtic's Frank McAvennie - all red-carded and later summoned by the courts, along with Rangers' Graham Roberts, to answer 'breach of the peace' charges. Thankfully, the game ended with honours even.

August 27 1988
RANGERS 5 CELTIC 1

Having just won the double, Celtic went into the first Old Firm clash of the season full of confidence and even took the lead through Frank McAvennie. But perhaps the visitors were guilty of being over-confident as Rangers romped to victory with goals from Ally McCoist (2), Ray Wilkins, Kevin Drinkell and Mark Walters.

November 21 1998
CELTIC 5 RANGERS 1

Two goals apiece from Henrik Larsson and Lubo Moravcik - plus another from teenage sensation Mark Burchill - earned Celtic a memorable victory at Parkhead. Rangers picked up yet another title come the end of the season but at least Celtic fans had the consolation of this emphatic victory.

ENGLAND 2000

SKY SPORTS

SKY SPORTS
SPEED ZONE

FEATURING: THE NATION'S FAVOURITE, CARL FOGARTY, PLUS BEST OF THE TRACK ACTION

FOGGY OFF THE TRACK

CARL'S WIFE Michaela has revealed that while the Superbike ace operates like a dream on the track; he's a nightmare off it – especially when he's injured, as he was for a lengthy spell after his bad spill last season.

All laid up and nowhere to go, Foggy was 'like a sparrow with a broken wing' and Michaela recalls how he used to try and overcome his boredom by constantly winding her up with his childish pranks.

She explains: "He went through an aggravating stage; like picking his toenails and stuffing them in my trainers, or burning me with a spoon after he's been stirring the tea or coffee." Charming!

As part of the rehabilitation programme, Michaela tried to get Carl to exercise in the family swimming pool; but found him an unwilling patient.

"He was an absolute joke," she says. "He sat there, chattered his teeth a little bit, shivered and went all goosebumpy. He said he didn't like it, turned round and got back out again. I wouldn't mind but the pool was up to 28 degrees. He was really hard work and drove me mad for a time."

Michaela added that Foggy received many 'get well' messages – including one from the great Barry Sheene – and, through his own website, he thanked everyone.

FOGGY: back on track

ALTHOUGH he was unable to compete at Donington, Carl Fogarty made the effort to greet his well wishers by making a lap of the circuit in an open-top car.

Fogarty lives close to the track in the middle of the British countryside, and considers it to be his 'home' circuit. Record numbers of fans every year flock to Donington to see their WSBK hero race.

The lap of the track gave spectators a chance to see Foggy for the first time after his unfortunate race in Australia, where he broke his arm; an injury which sidelined him until the summer of 2000 and robbed him of another title.

FOGGY: Four-time champ

Carl Fogarty has won the World Superbike Championship four times since 1994 and, but for injury, would probably have added title number five to the list last year. Here is how he's won his four crowns to date:-

1994

Wins: GB Race 1; Spain Races 1 & 2; Austria Races 1 & 2; Indonesia Race 2; Holland Races 1 & 2; San Marino Race 2; Austria Race 1.
Total Wins: 10 (3 doubles)
Six Poles: Spain, Austria, Indonesia, Holland, San Marino, Europe (Brands Hatch)

1995

Wins: Germany Races 1 & 2; GB Races 1 & 2; San Marino Race 1; Spain Race 2; Austria Race 1; Europe (Brands Hatch) Races 1 & 2; Japan Race 2; Holland Races 1 & 2; Indonesia Race 1.
Total Wins: 13 (4 doubles)
Four Poles: Italy, GB, Europe (Brands Hatch), Japan.

1998

Wins: Austria Race 1; Spain Race 2; Holland Race 2.
Total Wins: 3 (0 doubles)
No Poles

1999

Wins: South Africa Races 1 & 2; GB Race 1; Italy Races 1 & 2; Germany Race 1; San Marino Races 1 & 2; Holland Races 1 & 2.
Total Wins: 10 (4 doubles)
Four Poles: Spain, Germany, San Marino, Europe (Brands Hatch).

Superbikes need more spice SAYS FOGGY

THE RACE for the 2000 Superbike title lost much of its spice once Carl Fogarty was forced to withdraw because of the injury sustained in Australia. Who says so? The man himself.

Foggy reckoned that, in his absence, leader Colin Edwards on the Honda had little or no opposition – especially once Noriyuki Haga was banned for a month after a second positive drugs test.

The four-time champion said at the time: "In 1999, there were three or four of us in contention. But last year there was only one or two.

"When it was Ducati against Castrol Honda, with two good riders each, it was exciting. But once I got injured there was only one guy capable of winning week in week out and that was Colin Edwards.

"I just wish I had been fit enough to get out there racing. They needed me to speed it all up again and make the Championship more of a race. It seems even the top guys are getting complacent.

"The Championship needs depth and it didn't have that. A few years ago it could have been any one of eight riders taking a race."

Finland's Tommi Makinen in World Championship form

LIFE IN THE
FAST LANE

The thrill of a speedway meet still brings the crowds in

View from above - of Max Biaggi

Katuami Fujiwara - riding high

Loris Capirossi - check out the position of that knee!

Racing for the flag - Carlos Checa

Britain's Richard Burns - a rally star in all weathers

EXTREME
ON THE

Any chance of a lift!

There's only one way to get down a snow covered mountain side - fast!

And they were only out for a Sunday paddle in the dinghy!

EDGE!

You don't have to be mad to do this...
...but if you are it helps!

FUN TIME!

ANSWERS FROM P18/19

X WORD

```
S   J   P       D O   B
A O V A L     C O R S E R I
L H   R T     D   C     I T
F I N N I S H   G R A N T S
O S   S   R     E   R   I
R O O K   P A R R Y       S
D N   M   P   S   C   V
    P U R S E   T H A I
B M   N   T   T A   N
L E E D S   O L Y M P I C
A D   T   N   S   M   E
C L A R E T   H O Y A N
K   L   R     N   N   T
```

NAME GAME

2 & 6 Ian Woosnam   10 & 3 Saurav Ganguly
9 & 8 David O'Leary   1 & 5 Tim Robinson
4 & 7 Egil Olsen

T I G E R W O O D S

WHO R U?

1 **Martina Hingis** (Tennis)
2 **Karen Walker** (Football)
3 **Laura Davies** (Golf)

MISSING LINK

1 Lewis **(Carl)**
2 Button **(Jensen)**
3 Harte **(Ian)**
4 Wood **(Keith)**
5 Paul **(Henry or Robbie)**
6 Knight **(Nick)**

CRYPTIC QUIZ

Shane **WARNE**   Mike **TYSON**
ERNIE Els   Doug **ELLIS**
LEEDS Rhinos   **ROCKET**

W E L T E R

FIGHT ZONE

FEATURING: LENNOX LEWIS TRIBUTE... IAN DARKE'S FAVOURITE FIGHTERS... ACTION FROM THE CRAZY WORLD OF WWF

IT MAY surprise fight fans to discover that Mike Tyson does not figure in Ian's top six fighters from the last ten years; but there's a good reason for that. Sky Sports' main man ringside reckons Iron Mike was at his best between 1986 and 1990, so therefore doesn't figure. But these guys do....

No.1 EVANDER HOLYFIELD

Equalled Muhammad Ali's record of winning the world heavyweight title three times (and it could be four by the time you read this). More than that, he has figured in a series of fantastic fights throughout the 1990s; including three with Riddick Bowe and those two encounters with Mike Tyson. The measure of a 'great' fighter is the number of 'great' fights he has featured in and Holyfield, a modern-day gladiator, has starred in many.

No.2 ROY JONES

The supreme light heavy-weight in the world, Jones has an outrageous level of talent; combining phenomenal speed with a wonderful array of boxing skills. Apart from a rare defeat due to a freak disqualification, he has looked untouchable. We don't see enough of him here in Britain, which is a shame because he is absolutely top class. In fact there aren't enough fighters in his class at his current weight, which is why I would like to see him step up and take on some of the smaller heavies; like Tyson.

BOXING CLEVER!

TOP COMMENTATOR IAN DARKE SELECTS HIS FAVOURITE FIGHTERS FROM A DECADE OF SKY SPORTS

No.3 OSCAR DE LA HOYA

He is really the anti-Tyson; the golden boy of the sport. Having met him a few times I can confirm that he is every bit as charming as he appears. A great ambassadorial figure for boxing. In the USA, in particular, he draws in huge female audiences; not just because of his persona but because they appreciate what a truly brilliant boxer he is. The world champion at four different weights - and he's still only mid-20s - he says he wants to go on and win seven world titles. Don't bet against it.

No.4 LENNOX LEWIS

It has been a personal pleasure for me to cover the career of the first British-born boxer since Bob Fitzsimmons to become undisputed world heavyweight champion. There aren't many who have had that privilege. Faced with a torrent of abuse from America, Lennox defied all his critics at every stage. To the point that, while the Americans will never 'love' him, they do have a deep respect for him now. So much so that the American boxing writers voted him their Fighter of the Year.

No.5 JULIO CESAR CHAVEZ

The very embodiment of Mexican machismo, he was unbeaten in 90 fights over an incredible period of 13 years up until 1994. A world champion at three different weight divisions, he would have been higher up my list had we been talking about the 80s rather than the 90s. But he still figures very much in my thinking, and that of many others. Notably the 136,000 people who once watched him fight Greg Haugen at the Aztec Stadium in Mexico City.

No.6 PRINCE NASEEM HAMED

His glitzy antics are not to everyone's taste, but he proved himself over a five-year reign of domination - and 14 title defences - to become the undisputed, number one featherweight in the world. He has excited and caught the imagination of the so-called 'Generation-X' which boxing needs to do. 'Naz' wasn't the first to bring razzmatazz to boxing - his idol Ali did that many years before - but you have to admire this kid from a Sheffield corner shop who has made it to the top and is now respected throughout the world.

LENNOX
MORE THAN A DECADE OF DESTRUCTION

LEWIS Fight by fight

2000
MICHAEL GRANT	2nd round Knock Out

Retained WBC, IBF, and IBO titles

*Stripped of WBA title in courtroom in April

1999
EVANDER HOLYFIELD	12rd Unanimous Dec

Won WBA, IBF titles - Unification Bout

* Awarded IBO title

EVANDER HOLYFIELD	DRAW!!

Unification Bout, Retained WBC title

1998
ZELJKO MAVROVIC	12 round Decision

Retained WBC title

SHANNON BRIGGS	5th round KO

Retained WBC title

1997
ANDREW GOLOTA	1st round KO

Retained WBC title

HENRY AKINWANDE	5th round W

Retained WBC title

OLIVER McCALL	5th round TKO

Won WBC title

1996
RAY MERCER	10 round Decision

1995
TOMMY MORRISON	6th round TKO
JUSTIN FORTUNE	4th round KO
LIONEL BUTLER	5th round KO

1994
OLIVER McCALL	2nd round Loss

Lost WBC title

PHIL JACKSON	8th round KO

Retained WBC title

1993
FRANK BRUNO	7th round KO

Retained WBC title

TONY TUCKER	12 round Decision

Retained WBC title

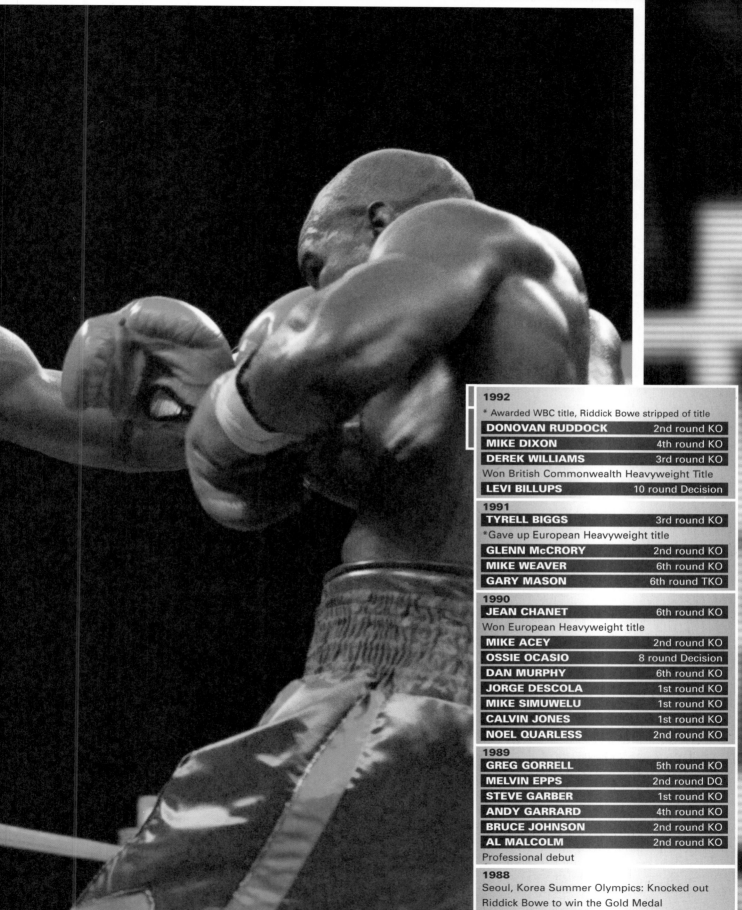

1992

* Awarded WBC title, Riddick Bowe stripped of title

DONOVAN RUDDOCK	2nd round KO
MIKE DIXON	4th round KO
DEREK WILLIAMS	3rd round KO

Won British Commonwealth Heavyweight Title

LEVI BILLUPS	10 round Decision

1991

TYRELL BIGGS	3rd round KO

*Gave up European Heavyweight title

GLENN McCRORY	2nd round KO
MIKE WEAVER	6th round KO
GARY MASON	6th round TKO

1990

JEAN CHANET	6th round KO

Won European Heavyweight title

MIKE ACEY	2nd round KO
OSSIE OCASIO	8 round Decision
DAN MURPHY	6th round KO
JORGE DESCOLA	1st round KO
MIKE SIMUWELU	1st round KO
CALVIN JONES	1st round KO
NOEL QUARLESS	2nd round KO

1989

GREG GORRELL	5th round KO
MELVIN EPPS	2nd round DQ
STEVE GARBER	1st round KO
ANDY GARRARD	4th round KO
BRUCE JOHNSON	2nd round KO
AL MALCOLM	2nd round KO

Professional debut

1988

Seoul, Korea Summer Olympics: Knocked out
Riddick Bowe to win the Gold Medal

CHYNA

It's fast, it's furious; it's downright crazy; professional wrestling 'American style' has been sweeping the States for the last two decades and now it's massive in Britain and across Europe too. Meet some of the characters and, over the page, check out some of the phrases commonplace in the mad, mad world of WWF.

TOP NAMES (and their real ones)

BLUE MEANIE	Brian Hefron
BRITISH BULL DOG	Dave Smith
BUH BUH RAY DUDLEY	Mark Lomonica
GRANDMASTER SEXAY	Brian Lawler
HARDCORE HOLLY	William Howard
ROAD DOGG	Brian James
SCOTTY 2 HOTTY	Scott Taylor
SERGEANT SLAUGHTER	Robert Remus
THE UNDERTAKER	Mark Callaway
X-PAC	Sean Waltman

THE GLAMOUR GIRLS

CHYNA	Joanie Laura
DEBRA	Debra McMichael
FABULOUS MOOLAH	Lillian Ellison
IVORY	Lisa Moretti
JAQUELINE	Jackie Moore
THE KAT	Stacy Carter
TERRI RUNNELS	Terri Ann Boatwright-Runnels
TORI	Terri Poch

Plus: performers employed just for television include:
MAE YOUNG, TRISH STATUS & LITA

HOW BIG ARE THESE GUYS?

BIG SHOW	7'0"
KANE	6'9"
THE UNDERTAKER	6'8"
THE ROCK	6'5"
TRIPLE H	6'4"
MICK FOLEY	6'2"
STEVE AUSTIN	6'1"
KURT ANGLE	6'0"
CHRIS JERICHO	5'10"
CHRIS BENOIT	5'9"

THE ROCK

WELCOME TO THE MAD, MAD

World Wrestling
Federation®

THE OLDEST

MAE YOUNG	79
FABULOUS MOOLAH	72
VINCE McMAHON	53
JERRY LAWLER	50
JIM ROSS	47
PAUL BEARER	46
MICHAEL HAYES	41
FAAROOQ	41
DEAN MALENKO	39
BRITISH BULLDOG & UNDERTAKER	37

THE YOUNGEST

JEFF HARDY	22
STEPHANIE McMAHON	23
TEST	24
MATT HARDY	25
TAKA MICHINOKU	26
SCOTTY TOO HOTTY	26
CHRISTIAN	26
EDGE	26
GRANDMASTER SEXAY, THE BLUE MEANIE, X-PAC & PRINCE ALBERT	27

* ages correct at time of going to press

THE BIGGEST EARNERS

STEVE AUSTIN	$6m (in 1999)
THE ROCK	$2m (in 1999)
BIG SHOW	$1m (per year until 2009)
KEN SHAMROCK	$1m (per year until 2001)
UNDERTAKER	$500,000-$999,000
TRIPLE H	$500,000-$999,000
MICK FOLEY	$500,000-$999,000
CHRIS BENOIT	$400,000
X-PAC, TAZZ, CHRIS JERICHO ROAD DOGG & VAL VENIS	$350,000

THE UNDERTAKER

WORLD OF WWF

A-Z of WWF

All you need to know about the world of wrestling

A is for ANGLE: A story line. Angles are what add to the soap opera element of pro wrestling.

B is for BIG TWO: The nickname given to World Championship Wrestling (WCW) and the World Wrestling Federation (WWF), the two main promotions in North America.

C is for CALL: Despite popular belief, the idea that wrestling matches are scripted move-for-move is false. Instead, wrestlers call their moves by whispering or muttering something into their opponent's ear, and from this the opponent will know what move he is to perform or be ready to receive.

D is for DARK MATCH: A match that takes place either before or after a televised event begins or ends and is not shown on TV with the rest of the matches.

E is for ECW: The 'Big Two' is sometimes extended to 'Big Three' to include ECW.

F is for FACE: A wrestler who is liked by the fans. Wrestlers are generally divided into two groups, the good guys (the faces) and the bad guys (the heels).

G is for GIMMICK: A persona that a wrestler is given to make him interesting. While gimmicks have always been a part of pro wrestling, from the mid-80s to the early-90s, gimmicks ruled in the WWF 'circus'.

H is for HEAT: Feedback from the crowd. A heel (bad guy) wrestler will try to get heat from the crowd by doing things to get them angry, such as cheating. If the heel has a lot of heat with the crowd, he is doing his job.

I is for INDY: Refers to an independent league. In the United States, all promotions other than WCW and the WWF are Indies, which have lesser known talent, significantly lower income, and usually promote in only a few cities.

J is for JOBBER: A wrestler whose only purpose is to lose to other wrestlers, so making them look good. The Rock's word 'Jabroni' comes from this term.

K is for KAYFABE: Simply put, kayfabe is the art of acting. When a wrestler 'breaks kayfabe' he is no longer playing the character that he is in the wrestling world. He is just acting like himself.

L is for LEMMING: In the 1990's, a 'lemming' was a name given to narrow-minded, biased fans for any promotion, not just the WWF.

M is for MONSTER HEEL: A term reserved for a select few wrestlers who epitomise all the qualities of a true heel. A monster heel must be the most dominate, fearless, toughest 'bad guy' in the promotion.

N is for NO CONTEST: When an opponent fails to show or refuses to fight. A walkover.

O is for OVER: If a face is 'over' with the crowd, it means that they cheer him. If a heel is 'over' with the crowd, it means that they boo him.

P is for PUMPED UP: Refers to a wrestler who is massive in size due to the use of anabolic steroids. If one wrestler says another wrestler is 'pumped up', he is basically accusing that wrestler of using steroids.

R is for REST HOLD: A move such as a chin lock or an arm bar that when applied allows the wrestlers involved to, as the name implies, rest. If applied longer than about a minute, it usually incites 'Boring' chants from the crowd.

S is for SCREWJOB: A finish that isn't clean, such as a wrestler being hit with a chair behind the referee's back and then pinned. Or when another wrestler or group of wrestlers run in and cause a disqualification.

T is for TWEENER: A wrestler (or manager) who is not a clean-cut baby face or heel, but rather, falls somewhere in between. Tweeners are generally created by accident, when a heel who is supposed to be booed is instead cheered by the audience.

V is for VALET: Invariably a female, who adds charisma to a wrestler's persona, and creates interest in male fans. If a wrestler is using a valet, 9 times out of 10, the wrestler and his valet have a private relationship in addition to their professional one.

W is for WORK: Simply put, wrestling is 'work' because it is fake but it tries to lead people to believe that it is real.

* There are no recognised phrases for Q,U, X, Y & Z. Unless you know different!

FUN TIME!
ANSWERS FROM P42/43

X WORD

	A¹		F²		M³				D⁴		L⁵		T⁶
	R	R⁷	O	A	D		K⁸	E	L	L	E	R
	S		E		R	U⁹		D	O		I		A
	E	M¹⁰	E	R	S	O	N		R¹¹	E	Y	N	A
	N		D		H	D		D	E		D		L
A¹²	B	O	U		H¹³	E	N	R	Y				
	L		M		W	R		S	D		T¹⁴		
			W¹⁵	I	T	H	E		S¹⁶	E	T	H
L¹⁹		H²⁰	N		I	I	L²¹				E		
E²²	W	O	O	D		L²³	A	M	P	A	R	D
E		R		A	L	P			N		N		
D²⁴	A	N	I	S	H		D²⁵	E	L	E	L	
S		S		E	S				Y		L	

NAME GAME

6 & 8 Kevin Wilson	1 & 10 Henrik Larsson
5 York	9 & 3 Eric Roy
4 & 7 Roy Evans	11 & 2 Lee Ashcroft

H¹	A²	R³	R⁴	Y⁵	K⁶	E⁷	W⁸	E⁹	L¹⁰	L¹¹

WHO R U?

1. Dennis Bergkamp **(Holland)**
2. Emerson Thome **(Brazil)**
3. Sami Hyypia **(Finland)**

MISSING LINK

1. Shaw **(Richard)**
2. Ball **(Kevin)**
3. Hyde **(Graham)**
4. Fortune **(Quentin)**
5. Sharpe **(Lee)**
6. Purse **(Darren)**

CRYPTIC QUIZ

Patrik **BERGER**	**NORWICH**
Dick **ADVOCAAT**	Matt **ELLIOTT**
Peter **REID**	Graham **TAYLOR**

B¹	A²	R³	N⁴	E⁵	T⁶

GIVE US A CLUE
ANSWERS FROM P70/71

1. Ian Wright	11. Jorg Albertz
2. Dave Beasant	12. Kevin Phillips
3. John Aldridge	13. Chris Sutton
4. Robert Lee	14. Alan Curbishley
5. Ryan Giggs	15. Mark Bosnich
6. Andy Clarke	16. Julian Dicks
7. Paul Jewell	17. Jim Leighton
8. Didier Deschamps	18. Shaun Goater
9. Joe Cole	19. Jamie Redknapp
10. Marco Gabbiadini	20. Nigel Martyn

SKY SPORTS

GREEN ZONE

FEATURING: GOLF'S YOUNG GUNS, TIGER WOODS v LEE WESTWOOD PLUS SNOOKER'S RISING STARS

DARREN CLARKE – Northern Ireland

Ryder Cup apps: 2 (1997, 99)
Highest Order of Merit position: 1 (2000)*
A respected match play competitor with a decent Ryder Cup record, his impressive victory over world number one Tiger Woods in the Final of last February's Andersen Consulting Matchplay Championship was a real confidence booster. It also earned him $1 million. After a slow start to last season, he won the English Open at Hanbury Manor before carding a 60 at the difficult K-Club (European Open). Has struck up a formidable partnership with 'stable mate' Lee Westwood in the Ryder Cup.

PADRAIG HARRINGTON - Ireland

Ryder Cup apps: 1 (1999)
Highest Order of Merit position: 7 (1999)*
The softly spoken Irishman emerged as one of Europe's great white hopes with a mature performance in the last Ryder Cup at Brookline. Has an even temperament and made an excellent debut, including a victory over former US Masters and British Open champion Mark O'Meara in the singles. He has a pedigree for match play having been a member of the winning Walker Cup side against the USA at Royal Porthcawl in 1995. Partnered Paul McGinley to victory in the 1997 World Cup at Kiawah Island and will be a key man for the European team.

PAUL LAWRIE - Scotland

Ryder Cup apps: 1 (1999)
Highest Order of Merit position: 6 (1999)*
The 1999 British Open champion has grown in stature since his famous victory at Carnoustie where he came from an incredible ten shots behind on the final day to win in a play-off. He made a superb Ryder Cup debut, forming a solid partnership with fellow Scot Colin Montgomerie, and picked up a number of points along the way. This included a brave 4&3 win over Jeff Maggert in the singles. Won from the front at the 1999 Qatar Masters. Had a quiet year though.

COLIN MONTGOMERIE – Scotland

Ryder Cup apps: 5 (1991, 93, 95, 97, 99)
Highest Order of Merit position: 1 (93-99)*
Europe's most consistent player of the last decade, Monty won a record seven consecutive Volvo Order of Merit titles during the 90s - but his lack of victories in majors put question marks over his temperament. Won five times on the European Tour in 1999 and retained his Volvo PGA Matchplay title last year. His experience from playing in the Walker Cup and five Ryder Cup tournaments make him an obvious choice for the Belfry showdown. Received an MBE from the Queen in 1998 and the European team will be looking to him to lead from the front against the US.

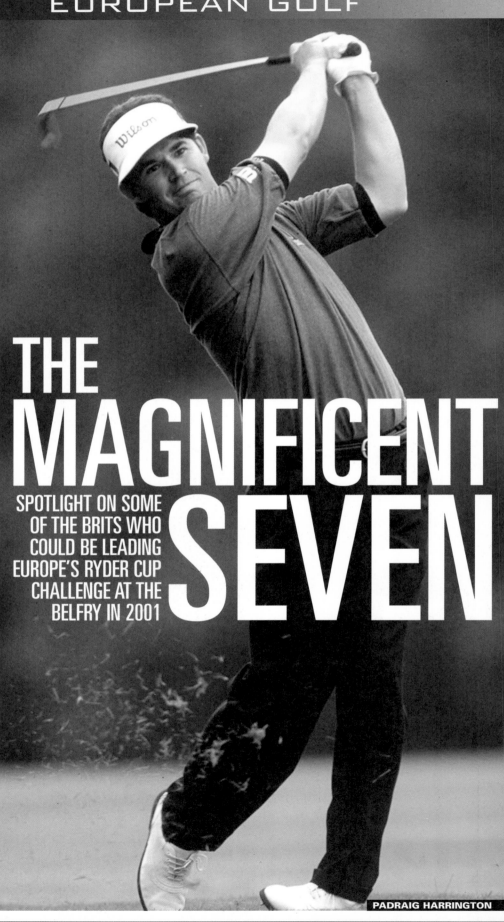

THE MAGNIFICENT SEVEN

SPOTLIGHT ON SOME OF THE BRITS WHO COULD BE LEADING EUROPE'S RYDER CUP CHALLENGE AT THE BELFRY IN 2001

PADRAIG HARRINGTON

EUROPEAN GOLF

COLIN MONTGOMERIE

DARREN CLARKE

GARY ORR

PAUL LAWRIE

PHILIP PRICE

LEE WESTWOOD

PHILIP PRICE - Wales
Ryder Cup apps: 0
Highest Order of Merit position: 6 (2000)*
Determined to shrug off his 'journeyman' tag, Price has been a consistent performer during his nine years on Tour, accumulating more than £1 million. Showed enormous promise after partnering Ian Woosnam at the 1991 World Cup when Wales finished second. But it took a further three years before he claimed his maiden tour win in the Portuguese Open at Penha Longa. He knows that the time has come to fully realise his potential; perhaps the Ryder Cup could see him do just that.

LEE WESTWOOD - England
Ryder Cup apps: 2 (1997, 99)
Highest Order of Merit position: 3 (2000)*
The Worksop wonder is one of Europe's most respected golfers, although his 2000 form has been patchy after 15 tournament successes worldwide in three years. Has enjoyed success all around the globe with wins in America, the Far East, South Africa and Australia. Westwood has been an integral part of the last two Ryder Cup teams making impressive contributions at both Valderrama and Brookline. Represented England in each of the last four Dunhill Cups.

GARY ORR - Scotland
Ryder Cup apps: 0
Highest Order of Merit position: 7 (2000)*
Won his first professional title at the 2000 Algarve Portuguese Open after coming close on many previous occasions. This included the 1999 Dutch Open where Lee Westwood's dynamic finish relegated him into second spot. Won the 1993 Rookie of the Year award after finishing 30th in the Volvo Order of Merit. Represented Scotland in the Alfred Dunhill Cup of 1998. No Ryder Cup appearances to date but few doubt that the potential is there for him to achieve great things.
* Merit positions up to summer of 2000

They will probably never be able to count 'Slimfast' amongst their list of sponsors and their waistlines might bulge almost as much as their bank balances, but Darren Clarke and Colin Montgomerie still rank among the best of the bouncing Brits.

Ask them to run a hundred metres and they'd probably run a mile (slowly!) but ask them to walk sedately around a golf course doing what they do best and the portly pair have what it takes to keep European golf's lightweights at arm's length.

Last year Clarke felt a million dollars after beating Tiger Woods, David Duval and a host of other top players at the Andersen Consulting World Match Play Championship, before going on to retain his English Open Crown – adding a few more grand to his swelling coffers.

At that point he was well on course for a million dollar bonus from his sponsors Dimension Data who promised him the seven-figure sum if he won four tournaments in a year.

Clarke had previously been accused of failing to live up to his enormous potential having won just five European Tour events since turning professional in 1990 – during which time he finished runner-up nine times.

The popular Northern Irishman admitted: "My swing hadn't really been good enough in the pressure situations, but that's all changed now – thanks to the work I've done with my coach Butch Harmon."

That and the confidence-boosting victory over Tiger and Co in the World Match Play, and Clarke said: "Suddenly, I felt I could win more regularly. I have much more belief in myself."

Montgomerie was enjoying the winning habit too, especially after landing his third successive Volvo PGA title at Wentworth and the cheque for £250,000 which went with it.

The win meant he was still some way behind bank-buster Clarke in the Order of Merit, but Monty was delighted with his PGA triumph, saying: "This is our flagship tournament and everyone wanted to win it. There was a lot of pressure on me after the first two days - the only way I could go was down.

"There were a lot of good guys just behind me, pressing, but three birdies in a row in the final round meant that it would have needed something dramatic for me to be beaten."

There wasn't - and Monty wasn't either!

HEAVYWEIGHT
CHAMPS
Clarke & Monty are best of the bouncing Brits

WOODS STILL TOP OF THE TREE
But Westwood can tame the Tiger

Sky Sports man on the course HOWARD CLARK SAYS...

IN TERMS of record and achievements so far, Tiger Woods is still the main man. But, while he is number one in America and Lee is just down the pecking order in Europe, there are strong comparisons to be drawn between two young men who could be going head-to-head at the next Ryder Cup.

For starters, their games are based around strong, straight hitting; the emphasis being on power allied to wonderful technique.

The number of times they find the fairway with huge drives on par-five holes is remarkable. That is where their strength lies.

They are both attacking golfers, both fearless when it comes to the ultimate challenge. Similarly, when hitting long irons on the par fours, they are equally adept.

Perhaps, around the greens, Tiger has the edge with his subtle use of the wedge but on the greens themselves there is little to choose between them.

When they are on a roll, Lee and Tiger are inspired putters. When the pressure is on they both tend to react in the best possible way.

In terms of temperament, they both have fire in the belly and an intense desire to be the best. They have the will-to-win all great players possess.

Their appetite for the game is very high and, as I said, earlier, they have no fear. Their public image, however, is very different.

Wherever Tiger goes, a huge entourage of bodyguards and advisors go with him whereas Lee doesn't feel the need to surround himself with so many people.

Another difference is that Tiger follows a strict fitness regime, often training for one-two hours each day. I don't think that sort of thing appeals to Lee too much!

Probably the major difference between these two great players is that, while Lee is always very relaxed about his golf, Tiger is very

intense; as we see all the time. Every shot Tiger hits is a 100 per cent effort and he seems to put himself under pressure from day one.

Whatever Tiger does he does 'flat out' and you rarely see him 'coaxing' a ball down the fairway. Lee, on the other hand, plays his golf without a great deal of fuss.

But, having said that, you can't fail to be impressed with the way that Tiger has handled the pressure and lived up to his reputation from such an early age.

He is one of the few players who have been built up to be something extra-special and delivered the goods...on a regular basis.

So many people before him, and not just in golf but in all sports, have struggled to cope with such a huge level of expectancy but not Tiger. Lee has not really had that.

As for the future, a lot will depend on how their early successes – and the pressure that goes with it – affects them.

TOP OF THE WORLD

BUT WILLIAMS DOESN'T EXPECT TO STAY THERE LIKE HENDRY & DAVIS

SNOOKER'S Player of the Year, Mark Williams, is a down to earth fella.

Even after his Embassy World Championship triumph over fellow Welshman Matthew Stevens his feet were still firmly on the ground.

Not for him the champagne celebrations and glitzy lifestyle which you would imagine goes with being the best on the planet in your sport.

After his victory at the famous Crucible it was straight back to business for the unflappable Welsh ace who, when asked how he would be celebrating, revealed: "I've got a League match at the weekend and then I'm working in the Pontins Holiday Camp for a week."

After that, a couple of months' rest from snooker, a bit of golf and time at home with his family in Wales. Far from the madding crowd.

"I tend not to go away anywhere, and just chill out at home because we spend so much of the season out on the road these days," he explained.

It's a little hard to believe then that the boyhood idol of this quiet, home-loving sportsman who prefers to shun the limelight was none other than the flamboyant Jimmy White.

Yes, the same Jimmy White whose lifestyle was every bit as energetic and unpredictable as his 'Whirlwind' nickname would suggest.

"Jimmy was my hero. I used to watch him on television holding up trophies with everybody cheering him on," said Williams.

"I used to think that it would be a great feeling to do the same but to actually be doing it myself is a bit frightening."

But even though Williams is at the top of the snooker tree at the age of 26, he can't imagine staying there for long.

He certainly doesn't expect to dominate the game in the same way as Steve Davis and Stephen Hendry have done in recent years.

"I don't think you will ever see that happen again. There are so many players coming through now that can win tournaments," he says.

"It is frightening how many players can win events now. There are 10 to 15 people good enough to do that and I am sure that the trophies are going to be spread around a bit."

Don't bet against Williams potting his fair share!

JOHN HIGGINS

STEVE DAVIS

New image for **SNOOKER?**

THE GAME'S rulers are committed to shedding what they themselves refer to as the 'waistcoat culture' by relaxing the dress code for matches.

Dickie bows out; denims in? Surely not. Yet something equally drastic was what snooker bosses were talking about as we entered the 21st century.

The fundamentals of snooker are safe but according to World Professional Billiards and Snooker Association chief-executive Peter Middleton the sport must come into line with golf and tennis in 'commercial and financial' terms.

Revealing plans to launch a snooker school of excellence, Middleton said: "We are competing for the same budget as other sports.

"I don't think we will be able to compete successfully unless we indicate to people that we are refreshing the game, are imaginative and are willing to change."

The changes are well overdue as snooker has never reached the peaks that it hit in 1985, when 18 million people stayed up late into the night to watch Dennis Taylor beat Steve Davis on the final black of the final frame of the World Championships.

With people like Mark Williams, John Higgins and Matthew Stevens around perhaps a return to the 'heyday' is not beyond reason.